Chakra Healing for Beginners

The Complete Guide to Opening Your Third Eye, Awakening and Finding Balance Your Chakra, through Guided Meditation

Crystal Stones

Table of Contents

Introduction

"Peace comes from within. Don't look for it outside of yourself."

Congratulations on purchasing *Chakra Healing for Beginners: The Complete Guide to Opening Your Third Eye, Awakening, and Finding Balance Within Your Chakras Through Guided Meditation,* and thank you for doing so. This journey through the chakras is your beginning to understanding what cannot be seen by the naked eye, and that is always a powerful force at work within.

Walking the path of healing can be a long and arduous journey, but it doesn't have to be. When you are looking for answers to your questions about working with your own healing path sometimes, it can be hard to find the information that you need all in one place, making your path toward recovery, healing, balancing and strengthening, even more, frustrating and complicated than it has to be.

My book, *Chakra Healing for Beginners*, will answer all of the questions you have and tell you everything you need to know in a fun, unique, and simple format. It will take you on that healing journey without any convoluted jargon or difficult to practice methods. This simple, complete guide is your answer to chakra healing, and as you read through it, you will feel like you are already making so much progress.

The following chapters will discuss everything that you need to know to begin your own chakra healing journey from the comfort of your home. You will learn what the chakras are and how they work, what chakra imbalances look like, as well as an overview of chakra healing basics. There will be plenty of information on methods that you can use to help your chakras awaken, heal, balance and strengthen including concentration and breathing techniques, tools like crystals, oils and plants that help the process, diet and exercise, yoga poses, opening the third eye, dealing with your past, and practicing the vibration of love.

You don't have to have any previous knowledge of healing your chakras to use this book. It is designed to be a beginner's guide so that you can work with this information from an easy-to-follow point of view and a step-by-step guide to help you unfold the beautiful, colorful, exotic, and amazing reality of the Seven Chakra System.

When you are ready to begin this impactful and transformative journey, this book will hold your hand and give you all of the powerful tools you need to commit to your chakra awakening journey. As you prepare to read this book, begin by imagining a rainbow of light in your body. Where your tailbone is, picture an orb of red glowing light and let the rainbow, going all the way up your spine to the crown of your head, transform from one color to the next. This is just the beginning of what you will see with the chakras, so let's get you started on the rainbow road of healing light energy!

There are plenty of books on this subject on the market, thanks again for choosing this one! Every effort was made to ensure it is full of as much useful information as possible. Please enjoy it!

Chapter 1: Understanding Chakras

Where are your chakras? Could you point them out to someone on a map of the human body, or on yourself? Do you know where they were originally discovered or what the word "chakra" means? What does each one represent and how can you tell they are even there? These questions are probably part of what led you to look for this book in the first place. Discovering the chakras is a wonderfully colorful and exotic adventure, and this chapter will begin your journey of understanding by answering these questions and more.

The Seven Chakra System may have originated in ancient times in India, but in our modern age, there are so many people who are learning about what this ancient wisdom teaches us about our energy system and how it corresponds to the rest of our bodies, including our thoughts and feelings.

You can learn so much about yourself and where you are currently in your life just by understanding what each chakra means to the whole system and what can happen when any of them are out of balance. To understand the chakra system and how it works, this chapter will break it down so that you can see the system as a whole and in parts.

Chakra Basics

The word "chakra" comes from the Sanskrit word that means "wheel" or "turning." Chakras are turning wheels of energy in your body. The term for them, as well as the study of them by this terminology, originated in the ancient Hindu religions of India. The Vedas, the sacred Sanskrit holy texts of that culture, described the meaning of the seven chakra system, how it functions, and what it does to open any individual to the enlightenment of the soul.

In India, the practice of Yoga also originated and was written about in these Sanskrit texts, and the practice of Yoga is strongly and directly linked to the energy of the chakras and the balance of all systems in the body through a series of poses and breathing styles and techniques. If you have ever been to a yoga class, you may have even heard the instructor refer to the chakras, but it is not always the purpose of yoga for people who practice to awaken and balance their chakras.

Chakras were originally depicted as wheels, or orbs, within the body that went from the base of the spine through the crown of the head. Each chakra was shown as a different color, beginning with red at the base and ending in white or lavender light at the crown of the head, passing through every color of the rainbow up the spine.

The healing journey through the chakras, according to Hindu beliefs, is what brought you closer to God or enlightenment. There is no religion, as you will see, continuing through this book, required to know, appreciate, and learn about the chakras. It is what they were inspired to teach their culture of origin that is important for you to recognize.

The concept of the chakras is that individually, they each represent a specific part of the self and are connected to certain mental, emotional, and physical aspects of the body. Separately, they each have a different vibration, tone, frequency, color, quality, and characteristics, and when you put them all together in a balanced way, they are wholeness on the level of spiritual energy. The wheels of energy are always in some kind of flux, either being open, healthy, and strong, or being stuck, blocked, stagnate, or imbalanced.

Think about your kitchen sink for a moment. When you turn on the faucet, energy in the form of water flows out of the tap and down the drain. It is a smoothly flowing process. When the drain is clogged or blocked, there is a back up of water that can't pass forward and circulate naturally through the pipes, which can be off-putting in more than one way.

Your chakra system is a constantly flowing form of energy within your body and when we are emotionally, mentally, or physically blocked by a variety of circumstances, issues, wounds, etc., our energy cannot flow freely the way it needs or wants to, leading to long-term issues, health problems, emotional disorders, and more.

The placement or location of each chakra connects to a number of physical aspects within the body and so when you are dysfunctional in your chakra system, then you will likely see some physical dysfunction in that part of the body. For example, if you have chronic aches and pains in your knees, feet, or hips, then it may partly be due to having a blocked root chakra.

Your root chakra is associated with your lower extremities and revolves around stability and security. If you are always experiencing physical insecurity and instability in your lower body, then you may need to look at what is blocking your root chakra. As you learn more about each chakra and what it relates to, you can interpret your body in a whole new language and way of seeing it.

When you put all of the chakras into a healthy balance through certain techniques, you are arranging their energies to be at their best frequency and resting state. Resting-state means "original frequency" and suggests where they need to be, or return to when they get out of balance. Your chakras will never be able to hold a resting state for long. Life's ups and downs, twists, and turns bring challenging shifts to our energy systems, and it is up to us to renegotiate balance from within.

The chakras are a matter of all levels of the body: emotional, mental, physical, spiritual.

The next section will explain what each chakra is and does so that you can see the finer details of what this system represents to your whole being. As you will learn, there are distinct differences between each, but they all need to be in a healthy balance in order for you to achieve true enlightenment and inner peace.

The Seven Chakra System

The Seven Chakra System will help you see more deeply into the aspects of all parts of your body from the root to the crown. As you read this section, take into account anything that resonates with you. Which chakra are you feeling most drawn to working with as you are reading? Your chakras will inform you of what needs healing, and listening to your intuition and instinct in these matters is a powerful part of what it means to have a balanced chakra system. Trusting yourself about your own healing journey is just the beginning of taking these powerful steps forward.

You may want to have a notebook or pen and paper handy with you so you can take notes about any ideas, thoughts, images, or emotions that might pop-up as you learn about each chakra. If something stands out to you, write it down. It may very well be the place you need to start your healing journey and chakra focus.

The Root Chakra (Muladhara)

The root chakra is the first chakra in the system and begins the journey. It is called red because of its frequency on the spectrum of light. Scientific studies aren't really being regularly performed to identify this possibility, but those who are engaged with understanding the science behind our internal energy system have done controlled experiments to effectively measure the vibrational frequency of the chakras.

The root has the lowest vibration, and the color red is also the same frequency, roughly. Other than color, the root is the first chakra in the whole system and is regarded as the seat of the life-force, also called Kundalini, that lies dormant in people, sometimes their whole lives, unless awakened. The spiritual, physical, emotional, and mental awakening that results from a rising Kundalini energy would take a whole other book to describe and can be an advanced course of study after you make it through this book.

The root chakra is connected to the lower extremities, including the feet, knees, thighs, legs, and the very base of the spine. It is also partially associated with the sex organs, but mostly with the adrenal cortex glands. The root is what regulates your ability to feel safe, secure, and stable and also relates to self-reservation. It can relate to financial security or the safety of feeling capable of survival. All wounds from childhood start in this root chakra center, and they extend out from there into other energy centers.

Do you feel like you are connected to yourself and authority with your life? Can you easily feel grounded and secure, or are you usually more anxious and nervous? Do you feel powerful or weak? A healthy root chakra means you feel grounded, balanced, physically well, secure, safe, and at home with yourself.

The Sacral Chakra (Svadisthana)

The second chakra sits around the area of the sacrum of the body, hence the name sacral chakra. It is below the navel and above the root, vibrating at the frequency of the color orange. This chakra is considered one of the three "lower chakras," including also the root and solar plexus chakras, which govern more of the physical reality of your existence.

The sacral chakra is about emotion and sensuality, as well as passion, desire, and creative forces. It is governed mainly by the sexual organs in both men and women, as well as the organs of the sacral region (i.e., bladder, colon, small intestines, etc.). Issues with these organ systems or with sex will revolve around imbalances in this chakra.

The sacral chakra is the place of creativity. It doesn't necessarily mean that you must be creative as an artist, as in with painting, drawing, or other artistic expressions. It certainly can be about those things and is a lot of the time, but it is also about the energy of creativity. Can you live your life, creatively? Are you able to be the artist of your life in unique ways, or do you box yourself in or follow the social and cultural norms that are prescribed? Do you go with the flow and express yourself through your own dynamic energy, or do you suffocate your emotional expression?

A healthy sacral chakra will allow you to feel connected to your sexual desire in a healthy way, your creativity to live life in your own unique way, your ability to connect and have intimacy, healthy levels of fertility, and a positive outlook about being expressive and emotive without being hyper-emotional in any direction.

The Solar Plexus Chakra (Manipura)

The solar plexus is higher up the spine, above the navel, and just below the breast bone. This energy center vibrates at the frequency of the color yellow and is often associated with the positive and affirming energy of the sun. The solar plexus chakra can be largely about identity, willpower, and self-esteem and helps you to feel connected to your purpose as a unique individual in this world full of people.

Because of where it sits within the body, this chakra correlates to the stomach, upper digestive system, and adrenal glands. It can symbolize the way that you physically digest fuel and energy into personal power. When people have a healthy solar plexus chakra, they are able to walk into a room confidently, share themselves with a group or community without ego-dominance, and can have a powerful ability to direct themselves toward their goals and ambitions without fear or personal criticism and judgment.

Overall, this chakra will make you feel like you are yourself and that you don't need to worry about what other people think about you. A healthy solar plexus is also generous about other people's need to be their own true selves, rather than being excessively domineering or overbearing.

Do you feel confident about your skills, abilities, and talents? Are you able to rationally and objectively judge your path forward so that you are only helping yourself meet your goals rather than putting yourself down along the way? Do you struggle with feeling submissive, or are you a dominant or aggressive person? Would you consider yourself able to achieve the things that you really want to in your life?

A healthy solar plexus chakra will allow you to feel in control of your habits, your life, your goals, and ambitions, forgiving of your mistakes and flaws with an ability to grow thoughtfully along your path. It allows you also to make room for others because you don't have to prove yourself to anyone and feel like you are one with your purpose and your true self.

The Heart Chakra (Anahata)

The heart chakra is the middle point between the upper and lower chakras of the seven chakra system. It is where the physical world and reality of the self meet the deeper spiritual energies, thoughts, ideas, attitudes, and beliefs of a person's whole being. The heart chakra is right in the center of the chest and is considered to be your energetic field that roams outside of your body by about 2-3 feet.

It has been scientifically proven that people have an energetic field directly pointing from their hearts and extending about 2-3 feet away from the body in all directions. The electrical impulses, rhythm, and beating of a heart cause this energetic field to occur. It makes sense then that we can be so easily affected in our heart center by either positive or negative forces and situations in our lives, knowing that our hearts are literally extending outside of our bodies to meet the world.

The heart chakra is the same vibrational frequency as the color of pale green. It is associated with the thymus gland as well as anything having to do with heart health, blood, and circulation. It can also be associated with the lungs, as when you are feeling heavy in your heart, sad, or low, it can feel difficult or challenging to breathe.

This chakra owns the concept of love. Alike in many ways to the intense feelings of the sacral chakra (sexual intimacy), the heart chakra is more about love in all its forms: brotherly, sisterly, platonic, familial, romantic, and love for all humankind and beings of the Earth. It is important to consider questions of the heart chakra to know if you are in a healthy balance and flow here.

Do you open yourself to love easily? Are you able to love yourself, unconditionally? Have you found it difficult to be supportive of yourself or others? Are you negative or pessimistic when good things happen to other people? Does it feel challenging to open up to people about how you feel, or are you open-hearted in general?

These are excellent questions to ask when considering the balancing energies of the heart chakra. Also, keep in mind that the heart is the bridge between the physical and the mind/spirit energy of the upper chakras. It is a powerful place and can also heavily stagnate and be blocked, wounded, and imbalanced. Opening the heart chakra can be a very powerful awakening for the other chakras as well.

The Throat Chakra (Vishuddha)

The throat chakra is the fifth chakra from the root and is located at the base of the neck in the place of the throat, resonating with the vibrational frequency of the color blue. The throat is associated with communication, speaking the truth, expressing yourself creatively and thoughtfully both verbally and in writing, and knowing when to be silent and just listen.

This chakra is connected to the respiratory system, organs of the throat, and the thyroid gland. Any issues that revolve around the neck, jaw, throat, vocal cords, and respiration will be connected to this chakra. The throat begins the journey towards expressing your true nature, purpose, beliefs, values, and philosophies about your own identity and reality. It can be a very concerning area for many who either feel afraid to use their voices or express how they feel or think. Conversely, for others, it can be a place of over-communication or oversharing, depending on the particular issues in some of the other chakras.

Your voice is unique, and it is the only chakra that can really explain how you are feeling, what you think, or what matters to you. If you have a healthy and balanced throat chakra, you will feel good about expressing yourself with others, connected to your personal truth, dedicated to honesty, and protecting the right to honor your purpose. It also reflects a balance of being able to listen to other people who need to also speak their own truth with their own unique voice.

Consider your throat chakra. Do you feel like you are able to talk about the things you need or want to? Are you honest to yourself or other people in your life, or do you have a tendency to lie? Are there times when you feel like you have to or are supposed to remain silent? When you consider what matters to you in your heart, are you able to talk about it and express it?

The way to become more open in throat chakra definitely revolves around saying what you need to say when you need to say it.

The Brow Chakra (Ajna)

The brow chakra is between and just above the eyebrows on the forehead and resonates with the vibrational frequency of the color indigo. It is also heavily referred to as the third eye and with good reason. The brow chakra, or third eye, is the center of your psychic awareness, vision, perception, intuition, wisdom, and cognitive abilities. It is in this place that the journey of enlightenment is able to go forward.

The brow chakra is associated with the autonomic nervous system, the pituitary gland, and the eyes, as well as the general feeling of well-being connected to wakefulness. It is in this chakra that all of our presence of mind, clairvoyance, psychic awakening and awareness, visions and dreams, and the capacity to look and see beyond exists. It is also a place of paranoia, hallucination, delusion, illusion, fantasy, and misinterpretation.

As with all things in life, there will usually be a positive and negative influence on any chakra. Blockages and imbalances in the third eye can make it harder for a person to truly awaken, and so it is here that many of us will tend to want to go first in order to prepare for the healing journey and the connection to our psychic powers.

In reality, it is most likely that other chakras will need rebalancing and strengthening before the third eye can be open and ready to "transport" you toward enlightenment. The brow chakra is brought into balance by letting go of cognitive distortions about yourself and reality. It can take a long time, sometimes years, to understand your perceptions and point of view from the place of the third eye.

A healthy and balanced brow chakra allows you to think for yourself, empower your intuition, trust your knowing, decipher and interpret messages and clues form the inner and outer world, and live very close to understanding your connection to yourself through all of your other energies. When it is good health, this chakra is a great "pilot" for the rest of the chakra system and the gateway to opening the crown chakra (see next section).

Ask yourself some questions when beginning to work with this chakra: Are you able to look beyond my fears, beliefs, and faults in order to see a bigger picture? Do you get lost easily in fantasies, or are you able to stay grounded in reality while you explore other dimensions? Do you get paranoid, confused, hypocritical, condescending, or prejudiced about things regularly? Do you feel grounded in your true-knowing about what is and what isn't?

In Chapter 9, we will explore further the power of the third eye and why it is such an important part of the awakening and healing process for your chakra system.

The Crown Chakra (Sahasrara)

The final (7th) chakra is the crown chakra, so named because of its position around and just above the crown of the head. It vibrates with the frequency of the color violet (others see it as lavender and even white light). It is connected to the energy of spiritual wisdom, truth, universal/ collective consciousness, and spiritual awakening. The crown is where you are beginning to let go of any and all misperceptions of the entire world and universal energies at play and at work.

There are thoughts circulating around the internet that the crown chakra is where you go through your journey, and it ends there- that once you have fully cleansed and healed this chakra, then you are done with your healing process and life will be a bowl of beautiful, organic cherries for the rest of your life. Unfortunately for those ideas, they are false and limiting to the growth journey. If you think it is over once you open your crown chakra, then you are still in denial about the work you have to do for your entire life to maintain and healthy spiritual consciousness.

The crown chakra is connected to the central nervous system (i.e., brain, brain stem, etc.), pineal gland, and eyes. Issues in these organs and glands can be directly related to serious chakra blockages and imbalances. A person can be too rigid in their thinking, overintellectualizing, and adopting cynical beliefs, behaviors, and attitudes as a result. It can also lead to an addiction to spirituality, staying out of the body and only looking at life through the upper chakras, when there is an imbalance.

The object of healing your crown chakra and practicing the work of becoming a whole being is that you find a connection to all seven chakras through the elemental and universal life force energies present and at work in all things. Balance can be hard to achieve, and for those who live their life skeptical of these things or who overanalyze the possibilities inherent in being an awakened person, they will likely not achieve healing or growth in the crown chakra.

The crown is not the end of the journey, and it will actually reinforce even more adjustment and rebalancing of all of the other chakras when you begin to activate your crown. It is a continuous cycle of recognition, strengthening, balancing, and healing. To understand how your crown chakra is doing right now, consider the following questions:

Does it feel like you are one with yourself but also the world and the reality you are in? Can you believe that you are not only completely infinite and energetically immortal, or are you certain that we all only live one life, and there is nothing beyond that? Do you feel judgmental of other people's, culture's, and community's belief systems, religious practices, or attitudes toward wholeness? Are you at peace with where you are in life right now? Can you accept that we are never going to be done with our journey and path toward awakening and enlightenment, or do you believe that there is a pot of gold once you find the end of the rainbow?

All of the chakras speak clearly about their characteristics and qualities. You can learn even more about their identities, structures, vibration, and energy when you begin to make contact and connection with your own. You will learn from your own seven chakra system what they are each like and what it feels like when they are operating well together as a whole.

To better understand the philosophy of the chakra system, it is now important to go a step further and explain why this attitude is a valuable aspect of understanding the human body as a whole. In our present culture, it has become more widely accepted that we are energetic bodies that are emitting frequencies at all times. But what does that even mean, and how does it relate to the chakras? The next section will explain more about all of that.

Frequency and Vibration: The Language of Chakras

The origins of the chakras came from a time thousands of years before now and were largely based on a religious doctrine from a specific culture. Today, chakras are being explored outside of religion, maintaining the Hindu (Sanskrit) name they were given in the Vedas of the Indic and Hindu philosophies.

Taking religion and culture out of the mix, when you distill it down to a universal concept, chakras are just energy. Energy is everywhere and in everything. No matter where you are right now, sitting on a chair, standing at a bus stop, in a coffee shop eating a bagel and cream cheese, everything you are in contact with is emitting a vibrational frequency. The chair, the bagel, the cream cheese, you, the napkin you use to wipe your mouth, all of it.

The reality is that energy, frequency, and vibration always put off some kind of wave, like a sound wave when you play music, only it isn't audible or tactile. Some people can feel and hear the energy frequencies of objects, people, and places, and usually, these people are highly sensitive and in tune with their own chakra system.

The seven chakras in your whole body are like a sound wave, emitting constant and consistent vibration at a certain, specific level. Vibration will occur on a spectrum of low to high, lower vibrations tending to feel more heavy, negative, dissonant, and dense, while higher vibrations feel more awakening, excited, light, delightful, and positive. It can be incredibly obvious when your energy and vibrational frequency shifts within any of your chakras. It will almost always change your attitude, thoughts, feelings, physical energy, emotional state, and patterns or cycles of existence, whether the shift is toward a lower, more negatively charged energy, or to a higher, more positively charged energy.

There are people who study frequencies in all kinds of ways, and it has only been in the somewhat recent past that researchers are looking at the connection between the chakra system, the human body, and energetic output or input. What we can see is that your energy system can connect to other energies and be transformed or altered.

For example, let's say you are feeling pretty normal and balanced, and then you enter a room where 100 people had just had a massive argument before leaving the room empty. As you walk inside, the frequency and energy of the room have been changed to reflect the negative vibration of 100 people fighting. The energy of your own body will immediately sense and feel that vibration, and even though you are not consciously aware of what happened in the space before entering it, you will begin to feel the shift in your own energy as it becomes overpowered by the low vibration of the room.

When you walk out of the room, you may start to have low thoughts and feelings. You could suddenly feel depressed and not know why. You might have a physical, emotional, or mental reaction to the change in your energy and not understand what it was, where it came from, or why it caused you to alter your state of positivity.

People all over the world have all kinds of daily activities and life experiences that shift and alter their vibrational frequencies in both directions. The power of honoring and acknowledging this allows you to understand where to begin healing your own frequency. If you have a negative attitude toward life all of the time and feel regularly low or depressed, there might be a handful of people, places, or situations that are causing your frequency to stay in a low or negative vibration.

The point of chakra healing is to help you open, awaken, heal, balance, and strengthen these internal frequencies and maintain their highest level of vibration so that you can live a healthy, happy, whole, and vibrationally high life. To be very clear, a vibration's "highness" has absolutely nothing to do with using substances. There are no substances (i.e., drugs, alcohol, prescription medications) that will actually help your body stay in high vibration or healthy balance. Chakra healing is related to changing your vibration through a variety of exercises, techniques, and realignments so that you can live your life without a need for substances in general.

There are several different ways that you can shift your vibrational frequency, and that is what this book is all about. Several people will want to know whether or not there is actually any evidence in science that can prove the effectiveness or truth behind the chakra system and how it heals. The next section will expand upon that.

Science and the Chakras

There are plenty of people who feel that the chakra system and the information about them is just pseudoscience. You could argue that those people have a blocked third eye and crown chakra, but let's keep it more diplomatic than that all around. The purpose of this section is merely to point out that there is always evidence that the chakra system is real and that healing your vibrational frequencies is possible.

In the scientific community, chakras are not something worth studying because they are based on religious philosophies, but when viewed from the perspective of vibrational frequency, there is much more "evidence" to support the concept of these centers in the body. As you read in the section about the seven chakras, the heart is proven to emit a field of frequency up 3ft or more away from your body in all directions. It can actually be measured and has been in several cases.

There are also people who study the concepts of energy, frequency and vibration and identify it in other ways, as in by using frozen water to identify the geometric patterns that are formed when water is exposed to higher vibrations and frequencies (*The Hidden Messages in Water*, by Masaru Emoto) or through the concept of watching sand transform its patterns on a metal plate while higher and higher frequencies are emitted (Cymatics).

You can find a lot of different studies being performed, and mainstream science is much quicker to judge the concepts because all of the evidence that chakra healing and balancing works come from personal experience and testimonials from people who have explored the possibilities of chakra cleansing and strengthening. Controlled studies are only just now on the verge of being performed, and a lot of that has to do with changing the language (from chakra to frequency) and viewing it as a more universal concept rather than the spiritual doctrine of Eastern religious culture.

As our world culture continues to embrace new meanings in all things through the use of spreading knowledge through technology, we are more and more able to understand how many people have actually had their own experiences with chakra healing. Many will post information about it in blogs or web pages to help other people who are searching for answers on their path.

Chakras are simply energy, and they are connected to your whole being. You can say frequency, energy center, vibrational feeling, or whatever else seems an accurate description to you. You don't have to believe in the religious background of where the term originated from, and it is even true that other cultures have their own terms or phrase to describe this type of energy. In China and Traditional Chinese Medicine, Qi (chi) is the word to describe the life force energy that flows through you. Other Western cultures might use the word "light" instead.

No matter what you call it, it is simply put energy. Energy is real and can be scientifically measured in a number of ways. Moving into the next chapter, let's take a look at what causes chakra imbalances and understanding how to interpret them.

Chapter 2: Understanding Chakra Imbalances

To better understand the chakras and how they can be imbalanced, refer back to chapter 1, and revisit how they can be healthy. When your chakras are out of whack, they will tell you, but you also have to be aware of how they are meant to be when they are in a good balance and vibration.

Giving yourself the awakening you ask for means answering to the information provided to you through your own energy. What does that look like? This chapter will explain some of the ways that a person will experience misalignment, imbalance, blockages, or excessive/ deficient energy in the chakras that can lead to a whole wide range of ailments, mental/emotional issues, and disorders.

Not all people will experience these chakra imbalances in the same ways, and so it is important to recognize that everyone has a different energetic frequency, body, mind, and soul. As you read through this chapter, make a note of what resonates with you the most about your own feelings and sensations. Where are you feeling out of balance in your life? What chakra does it pertain to?

And what are some of the best ways to consider handling those issues?

Symptoms and Ailments

Your body is a very elegant and complex machine. It is not just flesh and bone and mechanical engineering. It is not just nerve impulses and involuntary responses. It is also energy, and the results of certain vibrations of energy in the body affect your emotions, thoughts, spiritual essence, and your physical matter.

You can learn a lot form going to a doctor who will tell you that you must have some kind of chronic fatigue syndrome and that there really aren't a lot of cures or medications to assist that, only prescribing rest, healthy diet, and lots of supplements and water. What a doctor won't tell you is that you can change the energy frequency of your system to help relieve you of some of the root causes of that chronic fatigue syndrome so that you can remove it completely from your energy grid, in some cases.

Not all ailments can be cured by chakra healing alone, and if you need medical assistance, please use it in conjunction with what you learn in this book. Each chakra will have a different set of symptoms and ailments and if can confuse and connect with all of the other chakras in the body, creating a lot of cause and effect.

For example, you may have a deficient solar plexus chakra, which makes you feel inferior, weak, submissive, and lacking ambition. In this situation, the root cause of your deficiency in this chakra might also be caused by a block or low energy in your root, where your stability and infrastructure are supposed to make you feel secure and available to accomplish your goals because your basic needs are being met. If your needs are not being met and your root is blocked, it will impact the efficiency of the other chakras.

Let's take a look at each chakra again and briefly talk about the symptoms and ailments of each one can look like.

The Root Chakra

Feelings of unworthiness; emotional lack and difficulty processing emotional experiences resulting in long-held wounds, traumas, and suppressed emotions about past experiences; unhealthy relationships that are the result of having childhood wounds and insecurities that haven't been resolved; a harder time staying put in one place, growing roots, setting up home, feeling grounded, or finding sanctuary in a place; unfortunate circumstances repeating themselves in your life because of unhealthy choices being made from a lack of security and out of a need to survive; depression, fear, anxiety, distrust, guilt, shame, and an overall sense of feeling like things just won't work out, no matter how hard you try.

Some ailments can include eating disorders like anorexia or obesity, autoimmune diseases, chronic low back, hip joint and knee joint pain, foot problems, a tendency to fall or stumble and trip easily, weak legs, rectal problems, shooting pains in the legs, restless legs, varicose veins, damaged arteries of the legs and feet, edema of the legs and feet, arthritis, and muscle cramping. These physical ailments are only some of the issues that can arise. There are also mental-emotional symptoms of an imbalanced chakra, as seen in the above paragraph, and sometimes other symptoms and ailments that are particular to the individual.

Excessive root energy can mean that you are too focused on material gain and that you are also greedy with your wealth and abundance, as well as being influential in making other people feel ashamed for not having as much as you do. Deficiency in this chakra can mean that you are always wanting to spoil yourself and mostly when you actually cannot afford to do it, creating substantial debt and bankruptcy. It can also pertain to having a serious addiction to drugs and alcohol when there is a deficiency here.

The Sacral Chakra

Feelings of wanting to achieve creativity but lacking inspiration or spark; avoiding contact with others out of a fear of intimacy; delaying any progress in your emotional processes because you fear what will come up and would prefer to avoid the reality of it; enjoying a relationship sexually without wanting or needing to put any emotional effort into it; depression because you feel no joie de vivre; difficulty feeling aroused and wanting to hurt or blame other people for this issue; temper tantrums and emotional outbursts.

Some ailments can include infertility in both men and women, sexual addiction or sexual frigidity, bladder problems, kidney stones, lower intestinal disorders, pelvic cancer, prostate cancer, and vaginal cancer. Essentially, any issues that are connected to this area of the body will be affected by the energetic imbalance here.

People who have excess energy in the sacral chakra will have a lot more need to have sex and can develop a sexual addiction and will also have a lot more difficulty expressing their emotions in a healthy way. People who are deficient in energy in this chakra will have a much colder approach to life and be very closed off and even frigid. They will much more inclined to conceal emotions, but when they do express their emotions, it is usually after months or years of repression.

The Solar Plexus Chakra

Feelings of being overpowered or enjoying being the one who is overpowering someone else; challenges with self-esteem and expressing one's identity; fixating on other people's success and feeling envy or jealousy; adopting an attitude of self-importance, or an attitude that you aren't important at all; being overweight or having a need to eat excessively to create more energy in this chakra, or eating deficiently in order to starve the energy here due to feelings of weakness or worthlessness; giving up easily; ordering other people around and being dominating.

Some ailments can involve digestive disorders, stomach ulcers, acid reflux, kidney issues and renal failure, diabetes, drug and alcohol addictions, food and nutritional deficiencies and allergies, gall stones, and liver disease. The solar plexus region has some major organs that are all related to digestion and processing energy for the body to absorb. If you are having any issues in these organ systems, then your body is unable to effectively absorb and utilize nutrients, or energy which can lead to other health problems, as well as chakra imbalances, along the way.

People with an excessive solar plexus chakra will tend to be overbearing, domineering, egotistical, prideful, arrogant, conceited, jealous, envious, overly competitive, and also deeply insecure with low-self-esteem. People with a deficiency in this chakra will feel reluctant to try new things, afraid to be seen or heard, confused about their own place in the world, avoidant, submissive, meek, indecisive, disorganized, slow-paced, lethargic, depressed, moody, and fearful.

The Heart Chakra

Cold and distant towards others in general, or overly needy and suffocating; expectations of others of how they should feel about you; disconnect between loving someone and loving yourself; false attitudes or fake motions in order to please others; behaving like a martyr; judging large groups of people, cultures, or societies; avoiding affection; a sense of longing to belong; .

Some ailments related to the heart can be caused by issues in the physical heart. The heart is a powerful piece of internal machinery, and when the energy of this chakra is off-balance, it can really affect the function of the heart. People do feel "broken-hearted" on a physical level, and it is also an energy. Arrhythmias, high or low blood pressure, and other abnormalities of heart and circulation function can occur when you have a blocked or imbalanced chakra. Chronic cases of chakra stagnancy can also lead to different levels of heart disease. Lung problems are also notable here, including bronchitis, asthma, and also a desire to inhale smoke (as with cigarettes). Circulation of blood through the body is also an important consideration, and it can be affected by the way your energy regulated this important center.

Excessive energy in the heart chakra is what causes a person to feel emotionally obsessive, clingy, needy, and suffocating. It is usually out of a need to feel love when feeling like a person is not getting enough. This often occurs because of early life attachment disorders, which is also true of deficient chakra energy. People with a deficient frequency in the heart chakra will be aloof, stoic, cold, and challenging to get close to. There can sometimes be indications that the deficient person is incapable of loving anyone when really they are hungry and desperate for it underneath the façade.

The Throat Chakra

Speaking accusingly, deceptively, dishonestly, or not at all; avoiding verbal conflicts or chances to speak your truth; detailing things excessively; speaking too much or not enough; lacking an ability to listen to other people talk; talking over people; lying regularly or pathologically; challenges expressing your needs, wants, desires, emotions, or point of view; broad or gross generalizations about peoples or groups; raspy, thin, quiet voice; loud, oppressive, intense voice; vocal cord issues.

Some ailments can include lung issues, similar to the heart, like asthma or bronchitis. Other issues are related to the actual throat and neck, which might involve the chronic neck and jaw pain or tension, regularly occurring sore throats, coughing, difficulty swallowing, swollen glands in the throat, and mouth, canker sores, and so forth. A lot of the physical issues of the throat chakra are related to what kind of blockage or imbalance you are experiencing, whether it is excessive, deficient, or otherwise stuck.

Excessive throat chakra energy will cause someone to feel like they have to talk constantly while they are also not being a very supportive listener. In these cases, people will often make remarks that can be intentionally hurtful to someone else or will purposefully create conflict with a situation. A deficient throat chakra will indicate that a person is reluctant to speak their truth and that they feel safer holding everything in, despite this being very unhealthy for all of the chakras in general. Either excessive or deficient throat chakra can lead to any of the above ailments and symptoms, respectively.

The Brow Chakra

Being easily distracted or confused; fuzzy or muddled thoughts; difficulty processing your experiences or information you are trying to learn or input into your mind; forgetfulness; patterns of isolating thoughts and feelings and overthinking them; delusions and fantasies about people and situations in your life; feeling conflicted and not being able to make up your mind; fear of what other people think of you; grief for extended periods of time especially regarding your own lack of psychic ability; pretension about having a psychic ability.

Some physical ailments are connected to the brain, the eyes, the sinuses, and the pineal and pituitary glands. The Crown chakra also relates to the pineal and pituitary glands, both of which are in the brain and are responsible for excreting certain hormones that will regulate cycles and patterns in the body, like growth, sleep, organ function, etc. The effects of having issues in this chakra will exist mostly in the head, like having chronic allergies and sinus problems, poor eyesight or issues with the eyes, headaches or migraines, and so on. There may also be challenges with shutting off the brain to get rest and sleep or having issues with hormone balance in the body.

Excessive brow chakra energy can lead to a person becoming entirely open to paranoia, delusional and fantastical thinking, schizophrenia, dementia, having hallucinations, while also trying to explore and explain the psychic processes and practices of emotional and spiritual awakening. A deficient person will not be able to effectively connect with their intuition and will have a hard time knowing and seeing clearly, as pertains to clairvoyance and intuition. There can also be the rigidity of thought and lack of ability to think outside of the box.

The Crown Chakra

Overly intellectual about all matter in life; distorted views about how people "should" and "ought" to be or live; rigid thinking and close-mindedness; addiction to spirituality and trying to wake up your enlightenment experience without actually doing any of the "work" to truly understand what it means; depressed moods and dark thoughts; negative beliefs and attitudes about other people, cultures, religions, and backgrounds; avoiding the purity of thought that comes with a clear knowledge of the Universe.

Some ailments can relate to the function of the brain and will usually involve varying degrees of intensity. There are equivalencies between the brow and the crown chakras with regard to many of the mental disturbances that can occur because they are so close together and are very related to understanding the spiritual energies of life. There are many people who will elect to avoid their awakening and enlightenment both consciously and unconsciously because of the cost of not fitting into society any longer and becoming less likely to follow the rules. Fear is usually the result, and many people will believe that all of their physical issues have nothing to do with spiritual awakening out of that fear.

Excessive energy in this chakra can often be described as the quality of being arrogant about your thoughts, beliefs, attitudes, and knowledge. When you have too much crown chakra energy, you may believe that you know everything and will have a severe ego-mind that will take a lot of time to break down and balance. Conversely, deficient energy in this chakra will mean that you are unable to think for yourself and will just do what you are told and live by the rules imposed upon you by society and culture. You may also find it hard to have clear ideas and thoughts about anything.

This chakra also pertains to Universal consciousness and spiritual unity. It is incredibly challenging for a lot of people who are going through a significant life change to alter this chakra before shifting and rebalancing any of the other ones first.

Remedies and Treatments

There are so many different ways that you can begin to interpret and help heal these chakra imbalances. Not all ailments and symptoms will be treatable with the tools in this book, however, any medical advice or treatment that you are in need of can be effectively complemented by chakra healing work that you do on your own or with someone who specializes in this type of treatment.

The body is divided into four main areas: emotions, thoughts, body, essence. So basically, you have your emotional, mental, physical, and spiritual significance. All of us are consciously or unconsciously looking for a wholeness between these parts, and there is not one remedy or treatment currently that will serve all four levels of self. Remedies and treatments for healing chakra imbalances are varied and widespread across the globe. This book will show you many that you can do on your own at home, while there are also other therapies and treatments that you can explore that will require working with a trained or licensed professional.

Some of the self-healing remedies and treatments you will discover in this book are:

- Nutrition
- Physical activities, like yoga or hiking in nature
- Concentration and breathing
- Using crystals, oils, and herbal remedies
- Practicing letting go of past wounds

- Practicing love

In addition to these types of and treatments, there are others that you can find in your local community, and sometimes even online, that will help you do deeper with people who are trained to heal the four platforms of the human being. Some of those practices include:

- Acupuncture
- Massage
- Talk therapy, counseling
- Reiki
- Sound therapy (sound baths)
- Life-coaching
- Yoga retreats
- Mindfulness retreats
- Silent meditation

There are certainly a lot more options out there, and you will find in your search that there are plenty of ways that you can discover new tools for healing. All cultures have some kind of medicine-practice for each level of the body, and you will always know which ones feel best for you.

Side-Effects and Risks

The side-effects and risks of awakening and healing your chakra energy are a part of the cleansing and purging process. It is a process to go through energy shifts, and all of your energy changes in your chakras will manifest as emotions, thoughts, ideas, and physical symptoms. When someone is going through and energy purging and cleansing process, it can feel any one of the following ways:

- Flu-like symptoms
- Headaches
- Cold and sinus problems
- Achiness and soreness in the joints and muscles
- Tingling sensations in the extremities
- Painful memories resurfacing
- Emotional upheaval
- Emotional highs and lows, fluctuating between joy and depression and back again
- Awareness of things you weren't aware of before that start to bother you and make you more uncomfortable (i.e., personal relationships, living situation, diet, routine, etc.)

- Thoughts of suicide
- Coping mechanisms, like alcohol and drug abuse
- Confusion, disorientation
- Fatigue, exhaustion
- A need to sleep or rest more than usual
- Excessive hunger or thirst
- Weight gain or loss
- And more

There are so many different factors in the chakra healing process, and it will manifest differently for every person. We can always assume that we know what it is or why it is happening, but unfortunately, it isn't always an easy thing to interpret when you are going through the purging and cleansing process in your chakras.

The side-effects are not going to claim your life, and there are no real risks to choosing a chakra healing experience. The only thing you might have to consider is that you will need to be able to take good care of yourself, have plenty of time for rest and rejuvenation, and plan on going through a lot of emotional upheaval at random moments.

Benefits of Meditation on the Chakras

A great way to think about chakra healing is that it is simply a meditation on your energy. Your energy is a dynamic part of your existence, and when you are able to put a name, color, location, characteristics, and qualities to these energies, it can help you hone in on what part of your journey you need to be focusing on right now.

For all individuals, your chakra healing journey will be unique and incomparable to another person's, so it is best to try and focus on your own healing methods or approach and not worry so much about all of the other people's opinions about it. The point of this book is to inform and educate you about what the chakras are and why they get imbalanced so you can use the helpful tips and hints to guide you through your own healing journey.

Meditation is an incredibly beneficial way to work with your chakras. Your focus on a specific area of your body or energy system can help you pay close attention to how it feels, or what thoughts and emotions arise while you are connected to this place. Meditation is a general act of concentration and relaxation. When you silence your thoughts and turn off the world around you, there is a better connection to your inner energies so that you can hear what is truly going on under the surface.

As little as ten minutes a day of focused meditation can help you align with what your chakras are needing, and you can then travel further with your meditations and make them specific to the chakra you are working with at that particular moment. If you can ask yourself what is going on in a certain chakra, then you will discover answers as they come and will then be able to assess the quality of your current chakra energy.

There are meditations to focus on assessing energy, as well as awakening, healing, balancing, and strengthening the chakra system. The next chapter will expand upon those ideas and help you understand the simple basics of how to heal the chakras. Now that you have gained more knowledge about what chakra is and how it functions, you can learn more of the tools to understand the healing process.

Chapter 3: How-To Basics of Chakra Healing for Beginners

The journey begins with the basics of chakra healing. This chapter will cut to the chase and offer you a practical outline about how to heal your chakras. These subsections will illustrate the different levels of chakra work that you can engage with, followed by a simple meditation to help you get started with your chakra healing journey.

Use what you like from this section and also remember that your energy work is unique to you and will offer you the guidance that you will need the most. Learning from the positive side of your intuitive ability will help you activate each of these steps as needed. Let's get started!

Awakening the Chakras

Awakening the chakras is basically a call to action. They won't all be ready to come to attention and start shifting all at one time. The awakening process can take a while and will usually start in a major area of imbalance to help resolve other things later, like a domino effect. When one chakra is imbalanced or blocked, then there are at least a few others in line right behind it.

Awakening the chakras means bringing awareness to them and letting yourself know that you are ready to consider the reality of your internal energy. If you have been living your life not really thinking about it much, then your connection to your chakras is not very strong, and by practicing awareness, you will be more capable of aligning and awakening the energies within.

Awakening simply means "changing." When you are ready to awaken or change your energy, then you are ready to begin a great journey of transformation. Kundalini Awakening refers to this concept in the Hindu Vedas and that your root energy, the dormant life spark coiled at the base of your spine, is ignited and will begin to open each chakra going up the spine.

The path to awakening is long and will go in a variety of directions. It is rarely just one straight shot of uncoiling your force and awakening each chakra, one by one, up through your spine. You will bounce around and follow your own unique trail to enlightenment.

The basics of awakening the chakras are simple, and if you are ready to go on that journey, awakening is usually the first step. Remember, awakening is a way to create awareness. There are so many different ways to open and awaken the chakras, and truthfully, there isn't a "basic" or a "how-to" model to do it.

The best way to ignite awareness and energetic vibrational shift in your being is to create change. Change comes in all different shapes and sizes, and it looks different for everyone. The list below is just a sample of the ways some people will start their chakra awakening journey:

- Taking yoga or meditation classes
- Changing diet to be free of chemicals, processed foods, sugar, caffeine, and alcohol
- Spending more time in nature and away from large cities and towns
- Using crystals and gemstones on the chakras to shift the energy and help it ignite a transformation
- Going to a therapist to talk about your feelings and beliefs
- Asking questions about life through different philosophies or religious concepts that pertain to your journey
- Traveling to a foreign land and exploring the culture and scenery

- Revisiting your past with intentions to heal old wounds
- Giving up old patterns and habits to work on building and creating newer, healthier ones
- And more...

These are some of the basic ways that people may experience chakra awakening. For some, it is entirely spontaneous and will happen out of nowhere unexpectedly, sometimes from challenging life situations or circumstances, traumas, loss, or even drug and alcohol addictions. For others, it can be a very deliberate choice and will need instigation by making some life changes that will support your growth experience. Any of the possibilities from the above list can have a huge impact on your vibration and shifting it out of dormancy into "alive" mode.

Once you are ready to create awareness around your chakras and going on that healing journey, then you are on the road to awakening. After you begin to feel these large and sometimes small shifts in your consciousness, attitude, beliefs, and identity, you are then ready to connect to more of the actual healing journey.

Healing the Chakras

Healing the chakras takes time and patience. It won't happen overnight, or even over the course of a year. It can take a lifetime to really feel fully healed on all levels, and the thing about understanding your chakras and working with them to achieve your goals is that you will always be in some kind of a process with them, whether it is healing, balancing, or strengthening.

The healing process usually comes after awakening, when all of these stuck, toxic, and lower energies are shifting and transforming from whatever changes spontaneously or deliberately accelerated your opening process. The basics of healing the chakras are listed in this book in later chapters and will be continuously available and useful for balancing and strengthening the chakra system.

Healing takes personal work. In order to truly heal, you have to present and dedicate your time and energy to the process. The more you work with your healing process, the more quickly you heal, depending on what you are trying to do. Healing will evolve with you as you go through this process, and what that means is that whatever methods or tools you used to start your healing journey may not always work throughout the whole experience. Be willing to adapt.

Healing starts with awareness, just like with awakening. When you are aware of what needs healing, then you can process the emotions, mental states, and situations you find yourself in more proactively. An example list of how-to heal your chakras could look something like this:

- Use crystals and gemstones frequently to align, purge, and cleanse your auras and chakras by laying on the floor and placing them over the chakra for upwards of 1 hour.
- Visit a Reiki practitioner, or another energy worker, on a semi-regular basis to help you release and cleanse the chakras.
- Avoid situations and circumstances that are triggering or that will return you to the former energetic state you are attempting to heal from
- Continue seeing a talk therapist or other form of a counselor, whether it be a spiritual guide, life-coach, professional medium and psychic, shaman, or other, for the benefit of helpful guidance along the healing road.

- Practice meditation, breathing techniques, yoga, and other forms of relaxation and body release to empower the healing process
- Receive relaxing massage care and keep it on the light side- nothing too deep- so that you can achieve a state of deep relaxation where your energies are freer to heal and realign.
- Take notes about your journey and keep a journal of your feelings and experiences- putting it on paper is a very healing process.
- Change your diet to eliminate foods that leave you feeling overweight, or underfed.
- Adapt to a new self-care lifestyle that values your healing process before anything else.

These simple basics for healing are common for a variety of healing practices and regimens. For any chakra healing experience, the key factor is to create awareness and acknowledge how each chakra is doing, or which needs the most focus right now. Once you feel healed in a certain area, you will almost always be naturally guided to the next area of healing on the path.

This book will go into greater detail on the specifics of how to use some of these healing methods and tools, but the basics of how-to heal revolve around making time for it, finding what works best for you, and staying open to whatever comes up along the way. Taking good care of yourself and maintaining a healthy diet, lifestyle, and sleep schedule are essential basics of any healing process.

Balancing the Chakras

Once you have explored the elaborate ups and downs of the healing journey, you are now in a position to offer balance to the chakras by working to maintain them and keep them in a higher vibration, free of blocks and stagnation. So what does that look like?

Balance is a seesaw in life, and when you have an awareness of your chakras and how they feel when you are healing and awakened, then you can have a very clear idea when you are going too far in one direction or the other in some part of your journey. An example might be feeling upbeat, healed, rejuvenated, and able to have fun and celebrate your success and joy. Perhaps you are celebrating with friends, and you enjoy imbibing alcohol. After a few days of partying, you might recognize that you have gone a little too far, and one night of joyful boozing would have been enough.

Balance also means not living in extremes. It is helpful to avoid alcohol and substances while you are healing, awakening, and growing, but some use of substances can activate energy in certain ways, only when used medicinally and not recreationally. To recognize when you are no longer treating the energy medicinally, and you have gotten lost in the flavors of alcohol, or other stimulants is to choose balance.

Balancing your chakras can alter your energy and fine-tune it on a regular basis so that you don't go back to toxic levels of stagnation. Your energy will begin to shift and change in ways that you can't interpret right away, but over time, excess and deficiencies in certain areas will become noticeable.

So how will you maintain the balance and keep your chakras in a healthier state of healing and wakefulness? The balancing act will use similar methods from the lists above, like:

- Practicing meditation and mindfulness
- Maintaining a self-care ritual or routine
- Finding hobbies and crafts, or other activities and experiences that bring you joy and make you feel connected to your true self

- Writing about your life and what you are going through
- Eating and exercising intuitively, meaning that you will shift and alter your nutritional intake, or your exercise program to accommodate your current energy needs (for example: your solar plexus chakra is out of whack, so you change your diet to eat more citrus, vegetables, and lean protein and do your exercise outdoors in the sunshine, like walking, hiking, or biking)
- Performing self-healing meditations that will help you stay focused on your progress
- Getting plenty of rest and sleep
- Drinking plenty of water and herbal teas that are relevant to your current health needs
- Hydrotherapy
- Acupuncture
- Massage
- Counseling

Any and all of these tools and ideas can be effective with keeping your seven chakras in a higher vibrational balance after you have gone through the awakening, purging, and healing process.

Strengthening the Chakras

Strengthening the chakras will be more specific to each chakra and can be addressed depending on where you might be feeling the lack. This basic how-to heal step works well in conjunction with the balancing techniques in the last section. Each chakra has a specific need, and when you are honoring that need, you are aligning with and improving the energy of that chakra.

Lets' take it one chakra at a time for How-To Strengthen:

- Root Chakra

This chakra relates to earth energy and so can be strengthened by being outside in nature, going for hikes, camping, being close to woods, and forests, spending time in your garden, etc. It is the color red and so using the color red in your life more can be influential. You can also listen to the hertz frequency of 396 Hz and binaural beat meditation music with that frequency to help this chakra feel stronger.

- Sacral Chakra

The chakra of emotion resonates with the element of water. Spending time near or in water is very strengthening, as well as drinking plenty of water. You can use creative outlets that are specific to your tastes. Examples are painting, drawing, sketching, sculpting, singing, making music, sewing, crafting, knitting, etc. The Hertz frequency found in meditation tones and binaural beats for this chakra is 417 Hz.

- Solar Plexus Chakra

Fire pertains to the solar plexus, like the fire of the sun, and so feeling some heat is a great strengthener. You can take a hot shower or bath (also good for the sacral chakra), spend time in a sauna or sit in the sunshine for a period of time to absorb the sun's rays (use sunscreen as needed). Take time to do your own thing, especially if you are not used to creating time for yourself to be an individual. Dedicate some time to working on your goals and life dreams by putting them in your journal or on a vision board. The Hertz frequency to listen to for strengthening this chakra is 528 Hz.

- Heart Chakra

The heart chakra resonates with the element of air, and it can be very healing to practice some regular breathing techniques (yoga, tantra) to strengthen the energy of this chakra. Working in the community or offering your services as a volunteer is heart-strengthening, as well as contributing more time and energy to working on your own self-love process. Loving affirmations are an exceptional method for strengthening the heart (and other chakras). Some example affirmations are: "I love who I am every day no matter where I am in my process." "I love the people in my life and even the strangers I pass on the street because we are all human, and we all need and deserve to feel loved." The Hertz frequency that resonates with this chakra is 639 Hz.

- Throat Chakra

The throat chakra is related to the element of sound, and so it is helpful to use sound as a strengthening tool. You can activate your throat chakra by chanting, humming, intoning, singing, or speaking very clear and direct words of purpose, or affirmation. Channeling the sound of your voice is what you can do in order to empower your energy here. You can also listen to music or play music on your own. Writing and journaling will also be a very impactful throat chakra strengthener. The Hertz frequency for this chakra is 741 Hz.

- Brow Chakra

The brow chakra is associated with the element of light and asks you to go within to see your own inner light. When you are working with this chakra, the point is to awaken your third eye, which is your ability to see the world with your eyes closed. Practicing creative visualization is an amazing technique to strengthen this chakra. To practice creative visualization, you can simply close your eyes and picture an object or a specific place in your mind's eye. Practice seeing all of the details and fine-tune it as you look at it in your inner eye. Make it move, change its shape and size, give it a color. The more you practice, the easier it becomes, and the stronger your third eye will be. The Hertz frequency associated with this chakra is 852 Hz.

- Crown Chakra

The crown chakra is connected to the element of thought. For strengthening this part of your energy system, the best practice is meditation. To become strong in any part of your chakra system, you can use meditation, but the crown will have the most benefit from consistent and regular meditation sessions. It is helpful to consider your work in the world while you are strengthening this part of your consciousness. Are you serving your true-life purpose? Part of strengthening this chakra includes living purposefully and altering your life to accommodate that path. The Hertz frequency associated with this chakra is 963 Hz.

As you can see, each chakra has its own unique way of being worked with, and you can definitely see them separately while you activate, heal, balance, and strengthen them. As you proceed into the next section, determine which chakra you think you need to focus on first and use the following meditation to help you work with that energy.

Self-Healing Chakra Meditation for Beginners

This meditation can be used for any chakra. Simply apply the practice to the chakra you need to work with, considering all of its unique qualities and attributes.

1. Find a comfortable position lying down. Ensure that you will not be disturbed. You can play soothing music or light some incense if it helps you to find a calm and relaxed state.

2. Close your eyes and melt into the floor. Take a long, slow inhale and hold it for 2 seconds before releasing it.

3. Spend a few moments breathing out and in while you relax. Focus on the tension leaving your body from your head to your feet.

4. Once you feel relaxed, you can begin to put your focus on the chakra you want to heal. In this example, we will use the root.

5. Picture the energy of this chakra and its placement. Try to see if you can feel the energy when you focus on this center.

6. With your eyes closed, see the red-colored light of this energy center. Is it moving? Is it darker or lighter in color? Does it feel small or big? Spend some time considering this chakra in your mind and feel it in your body.

7. As you focus on this energy, notice any sensations, emotions, words, thoughts, or ideas that come up. Don't ignore them or push them

away; try to pay attention to what they are. They are likely energy stored in this center that needs to be released.

8. As these thoughts and ideas start to come up, picture the energy of these unwanted thoughts or feelings coming out of you. You can picture a vacuum cleaner sucking the negative thoughts and ideas away, or a wave of ocean water washing over you and taking away what your root chakra energy no longer needs. You can also perform an action of pulling the energy out of you with your own hands and mimic, throwing it far away from your body so that it never returns.
9. Spend time clearing your chakra and then return to your replaced breathing state for several breaths.
10. Now picture your root chakra and focus on it. Does it feel different? Do you feel differently? If so, how?
11. Return your focus to your breathing and either move to the next chakra in your body and continue with the same steps, or move forward with your day.

This simple meditation is an easy way to bring focus and awareness to your chakras. It is an easy way to engage with the energy and look for ways to connect with the information that may rise to the surface while you meditate. The more you practice this trick, the better you get at identifying what is coming up for cleansing, purging, and healing in your chakras. This can be useful for balancing and strengthening as well.

If you want to add a step to strengthen the root chakra in this example, you could picture the chakra spinning in a clockwise direction and get lighter and lighter in feeling and color as it rotates. You can picture a beam of white healing light coming from outside of your body and into this chakra to "charge it." There really are no wrong ways to meditate like this, so get creative!

The next chapter will offer another exciting meditation you can do to help you heal your chakras and will focus on the power of concentration and breathing.

Chapter 4: Concentration and Breath for Chakra Healing

Going forward from the last chapter, when you are working on healing your chakras, it is an invaluable tool to have a good grasp on breathing techniques and exercises, as well as powerful concentration. Both of these concepts are the basis of meditation, and this chapter will open you up to understanding what that means and why concentration and breath are imperative for the chakra healing process.

Your energy will always need a place to go and relax and when you can stop, focus on your feelings, and breathe, then you are able to connect with your energy centers in a way that will essentially block unwanted energies from causing a disruption in your balance, as well as helping your return to your center.

The world is full of upheaval and things out of our control, and these types of things are what throw us off course when we are finally just feeling aligned again. Breath and concentration will act as a shield from these outside forces so that you are regularly calling upon your own strength to fight for your own energy more.

You may have already learned a variety of yoga breathing techniques or tips for concentration and focus, and you should always continue finding new and exciting practices that work well for you. In this chapter, we will use a very simple, step-by-step activity to help you understand the power of breath and focus on your chakra system.

If you are new to meditation, then this will be a perfect entry point for you. If you are already practicing meditation techniques, then you are welcome to skip over this section.

Meditation for Breath and Concentration to Heal the Chakras

1. Find a space where you will be undisturbed. Silence your cellphone and put a do not disturb on your door, if desired (you can play meditation music if you prefer to start with some music to help you relax).
2. Find a comfortable seated position. You can sit on the floor with your legs crossed or on a cushion, and you can also use a chair if it is more comfortable.

3. Sit and take a few moments to adjust until you feel fully comfortable.

4. Make sure your spine is straight. If you are in a chair, be sure to keep your feet flat on the floor.

5. Place your hands comfortably on your knees, palms up.

6. Take an inhale in through your nostrils for a count of 5 seconds.

7. Hold the breath for 5 seconds.

8. Exhale for 5 seconds.

9. Repeat. In for 5, hold for 5, out for 5. Repeat this step 5 times.

10. After you have finished this round of breaths, concentrate your attention on your body starting at your feet. Begin scanning your feet, ankles, and toes for any tension.

11. When you find some tension in this part of you, take a deep breath in for 5 seconds and as you hold the breath for 5 seconds, picture the tension preparing to release from your body. As you exhale for 5 seconds, release the tension from your feet, toes, and ankles.

12. Move up to your legs (knees, shins, thighs, etc.) and scan for any tension. Perform the same action on the legs that you did in the previous step. Breath in for 5, collect the tension as you hold for 5, release the tension for 5 on the exhale.

13. Continue this activity through your whole body and use your chakras as markers of where to concentrate on releasing the tension. When you have made it to the top of the head at the crown chakra, and you have completed the tension release in all of the chakras, end the tension scanning in the shoulders, arms, and hands.

14. Breathe in for 5, collect the arm, hand, and shoulder tension while you hold for 5, and then exhale for 5.

15. Now that you have released the tension from your body, you can practice deeper breath within each chakra. The next series of steps will be repeated for each chakra, starting at the root and going up to the crown.

16. Take a long breath in for a count of ten. Hold the breath for ten. Then, release the breath in an exhale for ten.

17. Focusing on the root chakra, picture it in your mind as you take in the next breath for a ten count. See its color, light, shape, and size inside of your body.

18. Hold the inhale for a count of ten, and while you do, see the root chakra preparing to grow in size and clarity. See it getting ready to release any tension.

19. As you exhale for a count of ten, see your root chakra enlarge slightly as it pushes out any tension and unwanted energies.

20. Repeat steps 16-19 with the root chakra at least three times before moving up the spine to the sacral chakra.

21. Once you are ready to move to the sacral chakra, you can perform the same actions you did with the root chakra (steps 16-20).

22. You will continue these steps through every chakra, steps 16-20, moving up one more chakra after you finish your breath and concentration meditation for the one before. For the most effective results, perform steps 16-19 for each chakra at least 3 times or more.

23. Return your focus to your whole body once you have finished your breath and concentration meditations. Spend a few moments taking several inhales for 5, and release for 5. In for 5, out for 5.
24. When you are ready, you can return to your daily activities.

Using a breathing and concentration meditation like this one is a powerful tool to help you reorganize your energy and help you maintain all of the possible levels of basic chakra methods for awakening, healing, balancing, strengthening. It is simple, effective, and easy and won't take up a lot of time.

You can modify this practice and incorporate other, more yogic styles of breathing if you are familiar with some of those methods. Anything you do to bring additional breath and focus to the experience will be beneficial to you.

In the next chapter, you will learn the basics of how crystal, oils, and herbs are effective in treating the symptoms of a blocked chakra system.

Chapter 5: Using Crystals, Oils, Plants, and Other Tools for Chakra Healing

Energy exists in all things. Remember the coffee shop, the bagel, and the cream cheese? Energy allows you to continue to thrive in your life, or on the other hand, some energy can make you feel low, and like you will fall down instead of succeeding. Over the course of these pages so far, you have learned how vibration, frequency, and the chakras are all related so that you can truly understand why it works to heal the chakras from the perspective of shifting and transforming your energy.

So how do you shift and transform energy? Well, you have already read about the possibilities of breath and concentration and how meditation can bring you into a higher vibration. This chapter will share some other tools that will help you continue the practice of working with how your energy feels on a day to day level. When you are first getting started, you will probably not feel a giant change right away. Energy shifts are subtle, and they show up slowly as your body and chakra system process the shift that has occurred.

You will discover that there are a lot of tools that aren't listed in this book that will help you feel connected to your chakras and able to help them shift. Some of the most common and effective items are crystals, oils, and plants (herbs). It is truly amazing what you can do to reorganize your energy with these simple items. In this chapter, you will learn exactly how to do that.

Crystals and Gemstones

There are thousands of different colored crystals and gemstones all over the planet. They exist in a variety of places and are formed within the earth under pressure and through the combination of certain elements to make them what they are. The work you do with crystals is not hard or complicated in any way. They will do all of the work for you, and all you have to do is enjoy their company.

Each crystal and gemstone has certain properties and qualities, and you can find an amazing book of crystals that will give a full description of the healing properties they possess. There are many that are specifically used for healing the heart or the third eye chakra, while others are better for the solar plexus and the throat. There are crystals and gemstones for every chakra, and the reason they are associated with specific ones is because of that one simple truth: energy vibrations.

When you are using a gemstone that is specifically to help you strengthen your sacral chakra, you are using an energy frequency that helps that chakra awaken, balance, strengthen, and heal. It has the frequency that will almost match the original frequency of the sacral chakra, but it exists in the stone.

The same is true of other chakra stones and crystals so that you are able to identify the specific energies that you need in order to transform a specific chakra. There are also stones that are universal and can cleanse and heal all of the chakras. Clear Quartz crystal is one of the main crystals used that can be applied to working with your entire energy system. Another popular stone that is actually specifically for cleansing and clearing all of the chakras is blue kyanite.

Your choice of crystals will depend entirely upon your needs, so do some research first and decide what is going to resonate with you the most. You may also find that having a variety is good for your practice of healing and balancing. Having access to a variety of stones will help you stay at a healthy level in your energy, especially if you are keeping them readily available and using them on a regular basis.

You can apply any crystal or gemstone to your body during a meditation. Try using a chakra healing stone in the meditation from the previous chapter. Instead of sitting up, you can lie down and move the crystal or stone from chakra to chakra as you meditate and breathe. The impact and effects will be even more powerful.

You can also wear crystals as jewelry so that they are on your body or person at all times. It will feel refreshing to have them on you, and you might even notice a difference if you go for a few days without wearing them on your body. It may be a lot harder for you to maintain such high vibrational energy without them.

In the long run, having a selection of crystals on hand for awakening, healing, balancing, and strengthening is a wonderful addition to your chakra methods. You can sleep with them under your pillow to induce relaxed or lucid dreams, or put them in your bath water to charge the liquid with more energy. You can place them all around your home and office to help maintain certain energy in the space, which will, in turn, help the overall energy of your chakras.

A few crystals with you at all times can actually prevent you from getting too out of balance. There are those who feel that crystal therapy is a pseudoscience. However, the powerful frequency of crystals has been scientifically proven to conduct energy. A clear quartz crystal is piezoelectric and acts as a conduit for energetic frequency.

You can demonstrate the energy of your chakras in relationship to a crystal when you hold a pendulum above any one of your chakras. When you hold a quartz pendulum above your chakra, it will begin to spin in a small or large circle above the energy center. It will continue to do this until you remove the crystal pendulum form your chakra energy center.

The energy of crystals and stones will help you do even deeper cleansing and healing of your chakra system. They work best when incorporated into other methods, like when using them during meditation. They can also be used separately but will be most impactful when they are part of a whole healing program for your energy.

Essential Oils

Essential oils are commonly used for a variety of purposes, most notably for their aromas. Scent is a powerful thing, and a good smelling scent can do wonders for your mind, body, and spirit. In a lot of places around the world, people have been using aromatherapy to help people shift their consciousness, enter states of meditation, clear their minds, or their sinuses, and so much more. Every essential oil is made from a plant or flower and is essentially a distilled essence of that plant material, including the aroma.

Like a crystal, plant matter has a vibration and frequency, and so does an aroma or scent. When exposed to a certain essential oil, it can transform your energy very quickly. For example, when was the last time you smelled the aroma of fresh rosemary? Fresh rosemary is a traditional culinary herb, and when cooked, it loses its more potent scent but is an excellent flavor in many dishes. As a fresh sprig made into an essential oil, it is an incredibly eye-opening, invigorating, and brightening scent. It is commonly used to help people who are in need of clarity in their minds or upper chakras.

Any plant, herb, or flower that is turned into an essential oil goes through an elaborate distillation process that gives you a small amount of the plant's oils as a high potency vibrational frequency of energy. It is highly concentrated and, therefore, very powerful in scent and also vibration.

Essential oils can be used as an incense in a diffuser to help you shift your energy and can also be added to other oils to rub on the body. You can use a carrier oil, like jojoba or almond oil, and add several drops of essential oil before applying it to your skin or anoint the area of the chakra you are working with. Applying a small amount of essential oil directly to the skin is not unheard of, but it can also be irritating you may want to do a skin test before you apply it to a larger area.

The reason essential oils are so beneficial to changing your chakra energy is that they carry such high frequency but can also create immediate change by being inhaled through the nostrils having an almost instantaneous impact on the brain and the sensory perception that follows. Applying it to the skin can create a more subtle shift in chakra energy over time, so if you want the impact of the oil, use it for scent in addition to applying it topically.

There are many companies that sell a wide range of essential oils, and some will have a blend available for each individual chakra so that you can have the right formula for the energy of that energy center. Make sure you find essential oils that are using organic or pesticide-free materials. Anything that has been poorly manufactured, adding chemicals and other synthetic smells to the mix, will carry a much lower vibrational frequency.

Plants and Herbs

Essential oils use plants and herbs to create a highly distilled version of what they are and what they do. In general, plants and herbs have been used for thousands of years to treat a wide range of ailments, disorders, and even spiritual matters. You can use herbs to help your chakras work towards more balanced energy by incorporating them into your regular dietary routine.

A majority of people will make an herbal infusion, or tea, in order to enjoy the benefits of this energy transformation. When you imbibe herbal remedies, you are transforming your physical well-being, which is also associated with the way that your chakras perform. When your physical well-being is on track and in good working order, then your chakras are able to do what they need to do to give you the balance you are looking for.

It can happen for some people that a drastic shift and change in diet and herbal supplements can ignite a greater change and awakening of the chakras. As you are going through your own healing journey, you may feel naturally inclined to use more herbal supplements, teas, and remedies instead of other kinds of foods and prescription drugs. This is a normal part of the awakening, healing, and balancing journey that occurs. As you begin to shift your energy, you will naturally want a different way of life.

There are a lot of herbs available to you, and you will need to do some research about what kinds of herbs you will need for your own unique body and healing experience. There are a great number of herbal shops online where you can order sustainably sourced and organic herbs, or you can find places that sell them in bulk or packaged in your local community. If you are feeling really grounded in your earthly energy, you may even want to plant your own herbal garden in your yard to have on hand.

Herbs as a tea, supplement, tincture, or eaten as a culinary food or spice, can have a massive impact on the way that your body and your energy functions. Looking into an herbal practice asks you to be very curious about what each herb can do and how to use them. As you consider the options in using herbs, crystal, and oils, you will want to blend them together with your other healing practices.

The next chapter will take the herbal practice a step forward and talk about nutrition and physical fitness and what kind of impact both of these methods will have on your chakras.

Chapter 6: Nutrition and Exercise for Chakra Healing

Working on your healing process involves a lot of layers. It isn't just one thing that you do that helps you overcome your obstacles on your healing path; it is a variety of things all together that helps you to feel the way you want to feel. The way we work, play, sleep, and rest, all have major impacts on the frequency we carry. If you are living your life in a healthy balance, then you are likely to sense and feel when something is out of whack right away.

If you aren't used to living in balance, and you are accustomed to living as a person who hasn't paid much attention to spiritual awakening and personal growth, then finding a balance can take some time and a lot of adjustment. You basically have to reprogram your entire being to live in a new way. Part of chakra healing is that you are finding new ways to experience your life so that you can be healthy, whole, and happy. Questioning how you keep yourself whole, well and happy is where you begin to find out how your lifestyle is impacting or negatively affecting your chakras.

We all have our vices: sweet treats, coffee by the gallon, alcohol at the end of the day, cigarettes, and so on. When you look at all of these things as you are healing your chakras, you may begin to recognize how powerfully they can affect your energy and why it is important to face the truth about your body and your energy centers.

Let's take a look at the nutritional and exercise piece of chakra healing and how treating your body like a vessel of positive energy means taking good care of it from the inside out.

You Are What You Eat and Drink

There are so many different kinds of food and beverages available today. Everywhere you go, there are at least 5 to 10 different versions of the same bottled water, or soda, or bag of pretzels. The world is full of options for many people, and it will be a challenge in a world full of temptation to let go of some of the things that you are probably used to eating for pleasure, enjoyment, or because you think it is a healthy meal for you to eat.

Looking back to Chapter 1, recall that everything is energy and vibration. The whole point of healing your chakras is to help your entire being recover from a possible lifetime of thinking, feeling, and seeing negatively, or at least less than you are capable of doing. There is also a lifetime of possible food and nutritional deficiencies, as well as possible alcohol, sugar, caffeine, or drug addictions that can influence your overall mental, emotional, and physical state.

Nutrition is a controversial matter. We all have our own stories with food, and everyone has an opinion about what you are "supposed" to eat or not. The truth of the matter is that there are some universal truths about eating a healthy diet, including beverages, and that what you eat is literally what you are. Eating foods that are high in vibrational frequency will better feed the health of your chakras and keep them in a supported balance with your whole system.

Every "body" is different, and so whatever your dietary needs are will be of importance to you while you are working on your chakra healing path. The things that will help you stay on a healthy trajectory with nutrition and chakra healing are the following:

- Avoid alcohol and drugs, even prescription drugs, if possible.

- Reduce and/or fully eliminate sugar (it has a highly toxic impact on your body over time).
- Try to avoid significant amounts of caffeine and try using herbal teas instead.
- Avoid processed foods, especially anything that has a long list of ingredients that you cannot pronounce the names of.
- Avoid excessive amounts of additives and artificial flavors and/or sweeteners.
- Eat fresh fruits and vegetables, or cook them in a healthy way
- Eat healthy fats (avocados, nuts, olive oil, coconut oil, grass-fed butter, tallow)
- Give yourself a treat that you like every so often (once a month or every two) to avoid denying yourself
- Drink plenty of water
- Avoid sugary drinks, sodas, sweetened beverages, etc.
- Try to avoid fried foods and instead eat foods that are baked, steamed, or sautéed.
- Spend some time doing light fasting (e.g., eat in an 8-hour window and then fast for 16).

- Alter your portions to be a little smaller, or a little bigger depending on your hunger levels (if you are hungry, eat, if you are not, don't)

These tips can apply to any person, whether you eat animal protein, follow a vegetarian diet, or are vegan. The basic thing is to not eat artificial or processed foods. So many of the foods that are prepackaged and ready to put in your mouth are full of chemicals and products that have very little nutritional value for your body. It might taste good at the moment, and it might satisfy your hunger, but over your lifetime, it will only keep your energy at a lower vibrational frequency.

Choosing whole foods that are prepared in a healthy way will not only improve your physical body but also the energy of your chakras as well. The vibrational frequency of highly processed foods is very low and can be toxic to your system, especially if eaten regularly. You may want to consider eliminating them from your diet for a period of time, preferably about a month at least to give your body time to purge and cleanse the toxins that have built up in your system.

Making healthy dietary choices really does impact your healing, and if you want your insides to reflect the kind of energy that you want to maintain in your life, then choose your foods and beverages wisely. After all, you are what you eat.

Your Movement Matters

The human body was never meant to be sedentary, sitting down at a desk all day, or on a couch. We are designed to be active and to get the blood flowing. The concept of "getting fit" or "being fit" is not what I am talking about here. You can be very fit without looking like you go to the gym and pump iron five days a week.

What I mean is that *feeling fit* is the more important attitude, especially when dealing with healing your chakras. You don't have to work out all of the time in order to feel fit. You can do simple activities, like taking long walks or dancing around your living room. There are so many ways that you can move your body so that you are also moving stagnate energy.

Working on healing your chakras means looking at all layers and levels of yourself. The physical part of you needs just as much attention as the spiritual and mental part. Your physical practice doesn't have to be anything rigorous. Yin yoga is incredibly rejuvenating, and it is performed almost entirely while sitting on the floor, and yet it transforms your energy and stimulates a healthy chakra flow even though it is slow-paced and relaxing.

Physical fitness does not mean you have to be an athlete. Your movement matters, and as long as you are doing something, you are doing well. Your body is structured to move in certain ways, and even though a majority of people spend a lot more time sitting down than they used to for work or entertainment in front of the television, there are ways to create a healthier balance in the energy of your body.

The chakra system wants to be acknowledged by your movement. When you perform some kind of invigorating physical activity (e.g., walking, dancing, running, stair climbing, playing a sport, enjoying a hike in the woods), you are shifting your inner energy and your chakra system will change because of the fitness.

There is an old saying that if you are feeling blue, go out and get a little fresh air and exercise. It is scientifically proven that when you get your heart rate up and get the blood flowing, you feel higher in vibration or mood. Your chakras are always in an awakened state when you are using movement to engage with your physical body.

For most people, fitness and exercise are either a part of your life or not. When you are physically stagnant, your chakras tend to be also. It is a helpful way for you to keep your energy consistently flowing, and if you are using a certain regimen for exercise, then you are already off to a good start. If you are not, find something you enjoy and begin to slowly incorporate it into your life. Try doing some yoga once a week and see how it makes you feel. Put on your favorite music and break a sweat dancing. Go for a walk around your neighborhood every evening for 30 minutes.

You can also do things in the middle of your day that help you move more, especially if you work at a desk or have to sit down a lot. Take the stairs instead of the elevator. Schedule breaks to get up and walk around for 10 minutes. Whatever you are doing, make room for movement, because your movement matters.

Living Well and Staying Well

Chakra healing is a lifestyle choice. When you are choosing to create awareness about your chakra system, you are inviting yourself to stay wide awake to the possibility of making the changes you need to in order to live a healthier and happier life. That is the point, after all- to find your opening of enlightenment so that you can embrace how it feels to live as a balanced and whole person.

All of us are looking for our own unique version of that, and it helps to understand that we will all have very different experiences when it comes to healing our own chakras. The basics of chakra healing are all about looking at your own inner world to discover what you can do to create space for these little shifts and changes that add up to one big life change over time.

Chakra healing is an ongoing process that requires your devotion to searching for new meaning on the day to day level. It can be a very life-altering experience, especially when you are used to living your whole life up to this point a certain way. If you were raised on junk food, soda, and fast food, then you might have a challenging time shifting all of that into a healthier diet all at once. The same is true, too, if you have lived a mostly sedentary life. It can feel hard to create new life choices and habits that ask you to be more physically motivated.

The best you can do when getting started with chakra healing is to take your time and trust your intuition. Even if you are already on a healthy diet and going to the gym three times a week, are you paying attention to your intuition when your body says "less weightlifting, more yoga," or "fewer carbs, more greens right now"? Your body will evolve and change as you do, and your chakras will be right behind it all.

Asking yourself to be adaptable as you grow and shift your energy is one way to offer yourself a future of *staying* well. If you are choosing to live well and take good care of your body, and by proxy your chakras, then you are inviting the changes that need to be made and not setting yourself up for more challenges along the way.

Think of it like this: your chakras need what you are not giving to them now, and so in order for them to feel balanced, strong, awakened, and healed, you have to make the changes necessary to shift the chakras into their highest vibration.

Together with the other methods already listed in this book, the way that you eat and the way that you move your body will help you come to terms with what you need on a deeper level. Your chakras need to be nourished just as your physical body does. Your chakras also need you to move your body so that they can flow more openly and regularly, too. In the next chapter, you will learn about the significance of Yoga and its relationship to chakra healing. It will include a pose for each chakra to help you heal your system.

Chapter 7: Yoga and Your Chakras

Yoga is an ancient practice that originated in the same culture that the philosophy of the chakras did. It is a very influential body-mind-spirit practice that only became known to Western culture in the 1960s. Prior to that decade, the basic principles and practices of Yoga were kept by the Hindu gurus of India and taught only to students of that philosophy.

Several different styles of yoga have evolved over time, and now there are millions of people practicing it as a technique to help you stay not just in physical health, but also in mental, spiritual and emotional health as well. It is considered to be a "wholeness" practice. It is also true that the original concepts of yoga were designed to help a person reach a state of pure divinity from within themselves, often referred to as being a state of enlightenment.

A style of yoga specifically for awakening the chakras, known as Kundalini Yoga, has been regarded as one of the major sources of chakra awakening, healing, balancing, and strengthening. The practices and principles behind this particular style are geared towards lifting your vibration and ascending your energy so that your kundalini life force can resonate through all of your open channels (chakras) so that you may live your purpose.

All styles of yoga are, in essence, excellent for improving the energy of the chakras, and as you will see in the bullet-points below, yoga has a long list of benefits that are universal:

- Encourages and improves flexibility in the whole body (muscles, tendons, connective tissue, ligaments)
- When regularly practiced, it enhances the strength of muscles
- The various poses and asanas promote a much better posture overall
- The prevention of deteriorating cartilage and joints while aging
- Increases strength and flexibility of the spinal column
- Encourages and enhances healthy bones and has even been known to aid/cure degenerative bone disorders, like osteoarthritis and osteoporosis
- Increases blood flow and enhances healthy circulation, sending oxygen-rich blood to all parts

of the body resulting from the breathing exercise involved.

- Helps stimulate the lymphatic system which helps your body release toxins in order to promote immune health
- Encourages a steady heart rate for someone with either high or low blood pressure
- Helps to regulate gland function and hormone secretion
- Promotes happiness because of the release of serotonin and dopamine into the body
- In conjunction with a healthier diet and eating habits, yoga will lower blood sugar levels when regularly practiced
- Promotes focus and concentration
- Helps to improve physical stability and balance
- Helps promote relaxation and a healthy nervous system
- Relieves tension throughout the body
- Helps you to get better sleep at night because of it balancing and deeply relaxing abilities
- Can help with the improvement of digestion and related issues

- Pain relief
- Promotes peace of mind
- Helps to develop self-esteem and feeling good about yourself
- A heightened sense of self, inner power, and will
- Helps you get connected and stay connected to your intuition and inner guidance
- Can help prevent addictions and substance abuse, or maintain health in recovery from these issues
- Brings you into a deeper state of self-awareness
- Promotes self-care

The benefits of yoga are clearly impactful, and as you read further in this chapter, you will discover that you only need a few poses to really help you feel alive and awakened. The yoga poses listed in this chapter are meant to help each individual chakra come into fullness and balance, and they can be performed separately or all together as one chain of yoga poses to create a "chakra routine" that will go from the root to the crown.

Keep in mind that using your intuition is best when working with any chakra healing work. If you feel drawn to working with one pose for a lot longer or on its own for several days, then, by all means, work in that area for as long as you need to or as long as feels beneficial to your growth and healing.

As with any kind of physical activity, do only what feels comfortable. If you have to modify certain poses to be less strenuous until you gain more flexibility, then work within your comfort levels and work up to it over time. You can also find more offerings of various yoga poses and styles online that will give you further instruction and practice.

You can also go to a yoga class or studio and work with an instructor to help you find the right pace and path for your energy healing work. You don't have to join a class or a group, however, and you can learn the poses on your own at home and make them a bigger part of your overall chakra healing routine. Each of the poses listed can be done with a yoga mat, but you are not required to use one. It helps if you have a floor surface that feels comfortable for you to be working on.

Let's begin at the base chakra and build up to the crown. Wear comfortable clothing, and you can use a yoga mat or other soft surface to work on. As you will notice, the movement and posture of each pose will work well with the energy of the chakra it is meant for.

The Root Chakra and the Crow Pose

1. To begin this pose, you will want to position yourself so that your feet are a little wider than shoulder-width apart, toes pointing forward. Make sure your spine is long and straight. Picture in your mind that you are a tree growing taller and that as your spine lengthens, tree roots growing through the ground out of the bottoms of your feet.
2. From here, you will be lowering into a squat. This can take some practice to balance at first. If you need to widen your gait and put your feet out a little wider from your hips and shoulders, make those adjustments as needed. Reach your hands out in front of you to maintain balance as you lower into a squat.
3. Bring your arms into your chest and hold your hands, palm to palm, like you are in a prayer pose. If you can, try and tuck your elbows into your bent knees. Keeping your spine straight, you should be in a squat with your arms on the inside of your knees, hands in front of the heart.

4. Once you have the posture held, you can take a long, deep inhale of breath, followed by a long, slow exhale. Breathe into your belly rather than up into your chest. Make sure you completely empty your lungs before taking another breath.

5. Try a cycle of breathing like this five times in a row. You may need to stand up and adjust your posture if it isn't feeling right or if you are going to lose your balance, and that is perfectly natural and normal for a beginner.

6. Once you have held this pose for several breaths, you can gently fall back onto your bottom and sit. Roll backward slowly onto your back so that you are now lying down and take a moment to stretch your hips. Breathe and rest for several breaths.

7. Take a moment to listen to your root chakra and try to see if you can sense it a little more deeply than before. Spend time reflecting on the energy you feel in this chakra.

8. When ready, you can move your body into the next chakra pose.

The Sacral Chakra and the Bridge Pose

1. From a lying down position on the floor, lengthen your spine and make sure you are comfortable. If you have any low back pain in this pose, try placing a pillow under your knees.

2. Fill your belly with an inhale, breathing in through the nostrils only. Breathe in this way for several cycles in inhale and exhale. Focus on bringing your breath into your sacral chakra.

3. One you are feeling connected to your body in this area, start to pull your knees up by bringing the soles of your feet to the floor and moving your knees up so that they are pointing toward the ceiling. You will want to bring your heels in close to your bottom, but not so that they touch. Leave a little space and modify the distance for your own comfort level.

4. Keep your hands flat on the floor, arms down at your sides. If preferred, you can place your hands on your ankles and hold onto them for support.

5. Fill your abdomen with a deep inhale, and as you breathe in, lift your hips off of the floor and push them towards the ceiling. Go one vertebra at

a time, starting with the tailbone. Move slowly as you are breathing in.

6. When you are finished moving your hips and spine off of the floor, only your feet, arms, and head should be touching the floor. Try to get your upper back lifted off the floor as well, but if you need your shoulders to stay on the mat in the beginning, that's okay.

7. Hold this bridge pose for a few inhales and exhales before you return yourself back down to the floor. Make sure you are going slowly, one vertebra at a time on a long exhale.

8. Perform this routine at least a few times and maintain good breathing and slow movement. Try not to do it too quickly. As you perform this pose cycle more than once, picture your sacral chakra opening and getting lighter in feeling. Imagine what it looks like as you engage with this pose. Let all of the negative energy release as you breathe in and out and lift and lower your hips.

9. When you are ready, relax your body on the floor and lower your legs back down so that the back of your thighs and calves are touching the

floor again. Take a few relaxing breaths before moving into the next pose.

The Solar Plexus and the Platform (Plank) Pose

1. If you are starting from the previous pose, roll your body over on your mat so that your belly is now face down. Place your hands, palms down, in alignment with your shoulders and pectoral muscles.

2. Keep the tops of your feet touching the ground. When you are doing a traditional plank pose, the inclination is to push back onto your toes to lift you up, but in this pose, you will point your toes and leave the tops of your feet in contact with the floor. It will be a good idea to have a yoga mat or a rug for the comfort of the bones at the top of the feet.

3. Point your toes away from your body and try to maintain your pointed toes (like a ballerina) while you are going through this posture.

4. Inhale slowly and push your body up, as if you were doing a push-up, keeping your legs straight and your heels touching. Keep your spine

and neck straight. If you are not ready to do a full platform pose, you can do a half platform and simply push up from the knees instead of the feet, keeping your spine straight and your bottom flat.

5. Holding this pose, exhale and let your head slowly and gently drop down, looking with your eyes underneath you toward your navel.

6. Keep your spine straight while you inhale and exhale for several breaths in this posture.

7. When you inhale, try to pull all if the air down into your abdomen, filling it all the way before releasing it in and exhale.

8. While performing this routine, imagine that bright yellow sunlight is filling your solar plexus.

9. When you are ready to, you can lower yourself down to your knees and then back onto your heels, like you are curling up in a ball on the floor. This is called a Child's Pose.

10. While curled up in Child's Pose, bring your arms around behind you in the floor to grip your feet, forehead on the mat or floor. Stay here and breath for a little while.

11. Repeat the Platform cycle again, followed by Child's Pose, and repeat the full cycle as many

times as needed. It may take some practice to hold the Platform for longer periods, and that is completely normal.

The Heart Chakra and the Camel Pose

1. From the previous pose ending in Child's Pose, raise your body up so that you are kneeling on the floor. Position yourself so that your thighs and knees are in alignment with your shoulders. You should not be sitting back on your heels in this pose.
2. Place your palms on your low back, one hand on each side. Keep your shoulders relaxed and dropped.
3. Inhale deeply into your abdomen and chest. As you breathe in, push your heart center out, opening your chest wider and bringing your shoulder blades together. The action of pulling your shoulder together will help you open your chest more.
4. With your chest open, take a few more inhales and exhales, and with every breath in, try to open your chest a little more. When you inhale, be sure to fill your belly, pushing your abdomen out

as you inhale, rather than pulling the air up into your chest.

5. With another cycle of breaths in and out, try pushing your hips forward slightly, arching your back. With your hands still palms down on your low back, you can support yourself as you arch slightly. Try to get your heart center pointing more towards the sky.

6. Slowly and very gently allow your head to fall back so that your head is behind you, making even more of an arch with your body. Let your throat open and point up as well.

7. If you are flexible enough and feeling comfortable enough to do so, you can try dropping your hands from where they are on your low back and grabbing ahold of your ankles. Move slowly and do only what feels comfortable for you. You can build up to this posture over time with some practice.

8. Hold this posture and breathe in for as many cycles as you can. Try letting a smile emerge on your face while you hold this pose. If you need to go back to putting your hands on your low back and be a little more upright, that is okay.

9. When you are ready, release your hands from holding your ankles and slowly bring your head back to its upright posture, slowly returning to your original pose, hands, and arms comfortably relaxed by your side.

10. Sit on your heels and bring your hands together in a prayer pose in front of your heart chakra. Breath in and out for a few cycles before moving to the next pose.

The Throat Chakra and the Cobra Pose

1. Move your body so that you are lying face down on your mat. Place your forehead on the ground and keep the tops of your feet on the ground as well, as if you are going to do a Platform Pose.

2. Place your hands next to your shoulders, the same way you did in the Platform Pose.

3. Take a deep inhale in as you push yourself up, only this time you will need to keep your hips on the floor. Only your upper body will lift off of the ground.

4. As you enter this phase of the pose, make sure you are keeping your shoulders down so that

they are not hunched up in your ears. Keep your spine and neck long while you are pushing yourself up into this position.

5. You can take it a little further and let your hips rise slightly off of the mat so that only the palms of your hands, thighs, knees, shins, and tops of your feet are touching the ground.

6. Inhale deeply, and as you do, try to open or "puff out" your chest, like a cobra on high alert. You can also tilt your head back from here, slowly as you inhale. The point is to help you open your throat chakra, so you want to expose the front of your neck by tilting your head back.

7. Be sure to keep your shoulder down and spine long, and if you need to, soften your elbows so that they are slightly bent. Avoid overextending or over-straightening them.

8. Inhale and exhale, slowly and deeply, for several cycles in this posture. When you are ready, you can lower yourself down slowly to the mat, one vertebra at a time. Try lowering yourself on a long exhale.

9. With forehead back on the mat, breathe in and out a few times before repeating the pose

again. For optimal throat opening and cleansing, it is recommended to try this posture cycle at least 5 times.

10. Relax when you are down with your cycles and prepare for the next pose.

The Brow Chakra and the Pranam Pose

1. Begin by sitting back on your heels. If you need a pillow underneath your bottom, between your heels and your hips, feel free to give yourself that added support, especially if you have issues with sitting on your knees in this way.
2. Spend time breathing in this position. Breathe in through your nostrils and exhale through your nostrils. Allow yourself a time to connect to your third eye as you are breathing here. Hands can rest palms up on your knees.
3. Make sure your posture is straight, spine long, head in line with shoulders, while you are breathing. Notice your energy rising inside of you from the root all the way up to your brow.
4. Spread your knees slightly so that they are at an angle if you have not already done so. The

idea is to create space for your torso to lower down to the floor between your knees.

5. Breathe in deeply through your nostrils and begin to lower yourself forward. Keep your spine long and straight as you lower yourself to the mat.

6. Let your arms and hands reach out ahead of you like you are going to dive into water and swim. Try to let your torso touch the floor. If you can't touch the floor all the way, that is absolutely alright. You may need to widen your knees a little further to get to that place. Try to keep yourself very relaxed and loose in your muscles.

7. With your torso close to the floor, make sure your arms are pointed straight out in front of you. Pull your hands together so that they are palm to palm, with your forehead on the mat between your arms.

8. Hold this pose for as long as feels comfortable (ten minutes would be the preferred length for true transformation to occur). Keep your spine straight, and body relaxed.

9. While relaxing, focus on the energy of your third eye. See an indigo light pulsating and recharging as you hold this pose. Focus on your

intuition and spend time listening to any messages that come forward. Let your mind float and flow as you see visions in this trance-like meditation of the third eye.

10. When ready to leave this pose, gently pull your arms in and use them to help slowly and gently push you back up to a seated position on your heels or cushion.

11. You may need several minutes of breathing to relax back into reality. If you need to sit back on the floor on your bottom and bring your feet out in front of you, you are welcome to do so.

12. You can repeat this pose or move onto the next one.

The Crown Chakra and the Prasad Pose

1. You will begin this pose the way you started the last pose for the brow chakra (sitting back on your heels in a kneeling position).
2. Ground and center yourself with relaxing breaths in and out of your nostrils. Bring your focus to the energy of your crown chakra as you do this.
3. Pull your hands in a scooping or cupping motion toward your heart chakra, making a bowl

shape with both of your hands together. This hand cupping is where you can receive energy from outside of yourself, and it shows you that you are open to receiving higher vibrational energy from the Universe all around you.

4. Keep your body relaxed, soft, and focused on the energy of receiving Universal love energy through your crown and into your open hands. Breathe slowly and deeply through the nostrils for several breaths in this pose. Let a smile emerge on your lips as you inhale and exhale.

5. With your third eye open and wide awake, begin to visualize in your mind's eye, a beam of healing light entering your hands that are opened and ready to receive. You can also picture light pouring into you through your crown chakra and see that energy opening and uplifting your entire being.

6. Contemplate the energy of feeling enlightened by this Universal source of light and positive energy. Let it sill your whole body as you experience total wholeness and abundance.

7. Spend several minutes (10-30) in this pose and let yourself fully relax into receiving light and vibration into your hands and crown.

8. One modification you can do with this pose that is common for Yogis is to try "nose gazing." Nose gazing will connect you even more deeply to your third eye and further into the Universal consciousness of your crown chakra. Soften your eyes so that they are barely open and focus on the tip of your nose, looking only there, as you enter your meditative trance.

9. Keep your breathing going through the nostrils, long and slow, in and out.

10. When you feel ready to shift your focus back to regular daily life, start by lowering your hands to your knees so that they are palms up and continuing to receive. Spend time with your eyes open, breathing, and returning to the present reality of life. Start working toward standing up and take all of the time you need. Move gently and calmly out of your yoga routine.

All of these yoga poses are designed to help you move your chakra energy into a healthy and higher state of vibration and frequency. Put all together in one long routine. They will invigorate your entire chakra system and help you truly awaken, heal, balance and strengthen. You may also decide that you need to focus on one at a time for several days or weeks while you are working towards healing the energy of one specific chakra or set of chakras, and that is good as well.

However you decide to use these poses, remember that yoga and the chakras are cut from the same cloth and come from the same philosophy of healing and wholeness. It is the perfect physical, mental, and spiritual practice to help you feel totally aligned throughout your system.

For the next chapter, we will move away from the physical body and work more from the perspective of the mind and emotions. Everything is connected, and so even when dealing with the mental and emotional state of being, it is still greatly involved and imprinted into and onto your physical reality.

Chapter 8: Releasing the Past to Heal Your Chakras

Your past is not your present or your future, and sometimes we need to remind ourselves of that. In all of the chakra healing work you are going to do, you will find that some of the hardest work can be revisiting past hurts, wounds, and traumas in order to release them from your energy. You may not really think about it much while you are living your life or going about your routine. However, the wounds that we collect throughout our lives can really stay close and be long-lived energies that never really go away until we ask them to.

Your energy is always at work in your system, and when you are hurt by something, it usually doesn't go away after a few tears and some emotional challenges. Some wounds occur early in our lives before we even understand how to process our feelings or even comprehend what they mean in the first place. A majority of people alive today have had at least a handful of majorly important life moments that have left a scar or a mark on the mind, heart, and even the chakras, too.

Your energy will not work well if you are always hanging onto these wounds and traumas, and some of them are so deep that they actually become a part of your identity and the way you make life decisions and choices. When you are younger, you are in the care of your parents, caregivers, teachers, and others who will essentially mold your existence because of how they are, what they think and feel, and likely what wounds and traumas are steering their ships across the waters of life.

Early life programming happens on all levels and most deeply in the chakras. Your chakras are connected to your thoughts, feelings, and physical reality so that when you get down to the deepest platform of understanding your history as a person, you are looking at all of the energy stored over time that has made you feel less than yourself.

Energy builds up, too, whether it is positive or negative and when you are not dealing with the past, you let it live energetically in your system, vibrating at its own frequency and constantly informing you of who you are because of it, instead of who you are beyond it. Releasing your past is not something that can be accomplished overnight, and many people spend years in therapy trying to understand their thought patterns, emotions, behaviors, and beliefs in order to find the core energy of the self.

Healing the chakras is an amazing way to find that growth and release so that you can move forward, free of the energy from another time that no longer serves to help you feel like you are where you want to be living with yourself right now. This chapter will help you rediscover your past so that you can let it go for good.

Recalling Your Wounds

It may not feel good at first, and many people will avoid remembering the past because they don't want to ever feel that way again. As we all have learned as we have grown, the only way to make something better is to work it out by staring it right in the face. Avoidance will get you nowhere, and if you are trying to avoid your past, you are only going to block your chakras even more and remain in a state of low vibrational frequency.

You don't have to go over every detail of a past moment, experience, or childhood wound. You can just state the facts about it, or recall the feeling you had when it happened so that you are acknowledging it before you let it go. It is uncomfortable sometimes too, when you are going through chakra awakening, to suddenly be reminded of a past incident without trying to do so. It can just spring up out of nowhere in your mind, you will have a memory surface or a suppressed emotion, and you will not know why.

This is an important aspect of chakra awakening and healing to keep in mind. When you are consciously looking for past experiences to heal, you are mentally prepared to deal with them. When they randomly surface out of nowhere because of the chakra work you are going through, it can feel unexpected and shocking.

The best thing to do is to be gentle and tender with yourself. There is no harm in recalling your past. It might hurt for a little while, but the point is that you are bringing it to the surface to be healed and released so that you can make more room in your life for what you actually want to have. Releasing the past from your chakras isn't the same as going to a counselor or a therapist to talk about the issue, although that can certainly help and should be considered in conjunction with your chakra healing path.

When you are cluing into your energy, it will be more of a meditation on your past to help you identify it and understand how it is blocking you. For example, while in meditation on a chakra, you may have a few thoughts come up about your work life and how you felt ashamed when you got laid off. This would cause you to feel a lot of confusion in your energy if you never let go of that pain and you might live in fear of it happening again, or afraid to be better at the work you are doing now because you would rather do something you don't care about and get laid off, than do something you are passionate about and have your heart broken when it doesn't work out.

One moment in time is a domino effect of energetic results, and it can fall under a lot of different chakra energies when these things occur. In this example, your root, solar plexus, and heart are the most affected, but others will also be compensating for the blocks from the incident.

You might also have had a challenging childhood where you never felt fully loved or taken care of by your parents, having to look for ways to survive without knowing what it feels like to be truly secure. This will be a deeply rooted wound in the root, but also in the heart, crown, throat, and solar plexus. You can learn from your chakras as you go and giving yourself the opportunity to recall the wounds, spend time with them, and remember what they were, will help you in releasing them more effectively and deliberately.

Releasing Your Wounds

Releasing the wounds comes after you have recalled them. You can do this by using the simple meditation at the end of the chapter, and you can also use additional methods, such as seeing a counselor, journaling about it, or even opening up to your close friends and allies about it so that you can express through your voice (throat chakra) what it meant to you to have these past experiences.

The point is not to dwell on the past because when you dwell, you are clinging to the experience and then energy, keeping it locked in your chakra system. Releasing wounds will take some time to process, and so don't expect a miraculous change overnight. You might need several weeks or months, possibly years, depending on the situation you are trying to let go of.

There is no time limit for releasing the past, but it helps to move forward as much as you can as soon as you are able and to not linger on one past experience for too long. You will have so many other ways to help your chakras without focusing only on resolving past issues. They will come up naturally and will likely surface at the precise moment that your chakras are ready to release them, and this comes over time with consistent chakra healing meditation, yoga, lifestyle choices, etc.

To release the past, all you have to do is acknowledge it and give it a place in your reality for a moment, long enough to let it know that you no longer need it to be a part of your journey or your life. You can do this with the meditation at the end of the chapter, or if you are finding it difficult to let go of the energy, you can use affirmations to direct your past away from you.

Affirmations are an easy way to declare something to yourself. A few example affirmations for releasing the past are:

- I acknowledge that when [name past event or wound] happened to me, it caused me pain and left me feeling like I wasn't [name emotions or beliefs about yourself]. I am ready to let go of that experience because I feel differently about myself, and that time can no longer hurt me. I am stronger now.
- I will not blame [the person's name who caused a past wound] because they have their own issues to contend with. I am responsible for letting go of this hurt for my own healing journey, and I will not hold a grudge anymore. This grudge has

been toxic to my life, and I want to live from my heart instead.

- I release the [past experience] that I could not control so that I can make room for what I can control and for what I want to know in my life.
- I welcome new opportunities to grow by releasing the energy of my old life. I am growing and transforming, and therefore releasing and letting go.

You can modify these sample affirmations, or create some of your own that are specific to your needs. Letting go of the past is imperative if you want to truly heal your entire being.

Reflecting Instead of Regretting

Regret has a low vibrational frequency. When you are in a state of regret, you are basically staying in the past. You are choosing to live there, overthinking it, and feeling all of the "could have, would have, and should have" emotions that will keep you locked in low and negative vibrations.

Part of letting go of the past when you are healing your chakras is to help yourself move forward by choosing a mentality of reflection instead of regret. When you are reflecting on the past, you are able to objectively see the opportunity to learn from your experiences so that you can move on and forward into a higher state of consciousness.

Reflection helps you to identify what needs or wants to change in your life so that you are living more fully in alignment with your natural growth on your healing path of discovery. Regret holds you back. Reflection moves you forward.

When you are working from this healing perspective, teach yourself to reflect instead of regret and if you feel yourself start to go back to your old ways of regretting what happened, wishing you could change it or do it differently, or make someone else change it or do it differently, stop, take a deep breath and give yourself a reflective thought instead. Here is an example of turning regret into reflection:

"I regret that I never told my father how much he hurt me before he died. I am still so mad at him, and he should have known what he did to make me feel the way I do about myself today."

Transformed into a reflective statement is...

"I am sorry that I wasn't able to communicate with my father, who I truly am before he passed away. I would

have liked for him to see that even though he wasn't a great father to me, I was able to learn from him who I wanted to become instead of who he wanted me to be. I think that I can have peace with myself, knowing that I don't have to suffer any more when I am around him. I am glad he is finally at peace."

This shift from regret to reflection has a massive impact on the health of your energy, especially the energy of the chakras most wounded by the particular experience of this example. It is a simple and effective tool to help you leave the past in the past so you can be present with who you are today.

Meditation to Heal the Chakras from Past Moments

This simple meditation can be used on any chakra to help you release some past wounds and experiences. It may take practice to get closer to identifying what is rising up in your mind while you are focusing on the distant past, but try not to overthink it in the beginning. Let your feelings rise up; however, they need to. You may spontaneously cry, or laugh, or just feel really intense emotions. Let yourself feel them so that they can be released from your chakras effectively.

1. Find a comfortable position lying down. Spend some time doing some deep and slow inhales and exhales to relax your body.

2. Scan your body for tension and work your way through your whole body to release any muscles that might be clenched, tight, or tense. Breathe deeply while you release the tension.

3. Bring your focus to your chakras and visualize them in your body. See their colors and their positions as you look at yourself from within your third eye.

4. Spend time just being open to the chakra energy within you and hold this reflection for several breaths or until you feel directed to a specific chakra.

5. You may feel pulled to a certain chakra, but if not, you can just choose where you intuitively feel like beginning your past healing work.

6. Concentrate on the chakra that you are guided to and see its color. Spend time holding space for this chakra and think about what it represents. Meditate on this chakra for several breaths and let it show you how it is feeling.

7. You may need to lie in this meditation and reflection state for at least 10 minutes before you even begin to sense any energy coming up to the surface for acknowledgment.

8. You may begin to see images or past memories in your mind's eye. You could also have a train of thought that winds around toward a specific event or situation. You could suddenly feel like you need to let out some emotions through crying, yelling, or laughing.

9. Whatever rises to the surface, so your best not to stop it or block it from happening. The point is to create awareness so that you can achieve your goal of letting it go for good.

10. When you are dealing with this energy coming up for healing, all you have to do is let it happen. Don't try to force any changes or do anything specific. Relax your body and your mind and go with the flow. Let your chakras do all of the guidance and releasing while you just explore the experience.

11. Once you feel like you have had an emotional breakthrough or release, you can engage with your breath again. You may not want to work on

releasing any other chakra energies at this point and just give yourself time to relax and process your experience. It will be a good feeling to just rest after a catharsis or purge of this kind.

12. Repeat these steps as often as you need to in order to practice releasing energy from the chakras. It will always benefit you even if you are not clear or certain about what you are releasing. Over time, you will get better at "seeing" what is coming up to be healed.

Moving forward from this meditation and the concept of releasing the past, so much of the energy healing work that you do relies upon seeing it from your third eye. When your brow chakra is awakened and open, you are better able to see and experience the healing process. Since you are dealing with the release and balance of energy, it is only possible to witness it through the channels of the third eye.

The next chapter will help you align with the third eye energy so that you can begin to understand your own sensitivities to your energy and your psychic and clairvoyant connection to the world around you.

Chapter 9: The Third Eye and Your Psychic Awakening

The third eye is the main ascension space when you are preparing to reach enlightenment. You cannot begin to even wonder what it means to be enlightened if your third eye is blocked, congested, or stagnant. The third eye is the seat of perception, intuition, and "clear knowing," and it is how we are wonderfully able to connect to our dreams and visions in a more profound way.

You can live your whole life without ever knowing the quality of what it feels like to be connected to this part of yourself, and many people describe it as feeling high without having any drugs or alcohol. It can be the way that you ask yourself to pursue a higher mind so that you can live a fuller life, which sometimes means letting go of the status quo and not trying so hard to "fit in."

Answering the call of the third eye isn't as hard as people might suggest, and when you are open to it and have created awareness about it, you can begin to use simple tools to help yourself realize the power of the third eye in your overall chakra healing experience. This chapter will guide you through some simple tools and tips to seeing beyond what your eyes can see and waking up to another dimension of understanding yourself and the world you live in.

Mental Relaxation Tools to Awaken Higher Consciousness

Your mind is a machine, constantly computing and deciding, deciphering and learning, and even feeling skeptical or judgmental. Your third eye doesn't have time for all of that and will have a harder time being open if you are closed off to it with your mental thoughts. The third eye is energy, and it is the beginning of your worlds becoming one, between the physical and the spiritual.

The mental attitudes and beliefs that people adopt in early life, or adapt to within their culture or community, can be very limiting to the third eye and so as you prepare to work with opening this energy, it is important to find ways to relax your mind in order to awaken higher consciousness.

There are a variety of simple tools that can help you find mental relaxation, and in this chapter, you will only really need to focus on one concept: mindfulness.

Mindfulness is a form of meditation that can be performed in any situation. It is an act of being totally conscious of everything that you are experiencing at the moment without letting your mind wander too far into the past or the future. It keeps your mind free of anxious or worrisome thoughts because you are working only to engage with the experience you are having *right now*.

Mindfulness can take some practice, and it is incredibly simple to learn. All you have to do is follow these simple guidelines:

1. Focus and concentrate on what you are working with right now.
2. Don't get caught up in making assumptions or having too many opinions about the experience. Try to just enjoy a quiet mind while you take in the situation or surroundings.
3. Find the openings you see in your intuition and let them guide you forward. Trust your instinct.
4. When your mind starts to churn too much, or worry what others might be doing, thinking and feeling, return yourself to what you are doing and give it added focus.
5. Breathe, inhales and exhales, steadily and calmly.
6. Give yourself over to going with the flow and don't try to control the situation or the outcomes.

7. Visualize your inner world as it is making contact with your outer world and see how the two can be together. Practice seeing more than what your eyes can see naturally.

These simple guidelines are just some of the basics of practicing mindfulness. When you are working to incorporate a higher consciousness level of thinking and processing information, you have to be able to let go of control and just bear witness to reality. It will show you what you need to know, rather than imposing an opinion, belief, or attitude upon it.

This is the platform for thinking from a higher state of being, and it will naturally occur that your third eye will expand and become more alive to your overall thought process naturally as a result of this attitude or process.

The Art of Creative Visualization

To be able to see with your eyes closed is the gift of the third eye. It is not something reserved only for the enlightened. It is possible for any person, no matter what level of awakening they are involved with at the moment. All it takes is a little effort and a few minutes of your time to practice this useful skill.

Creative visualization feels a lot like what it is like to dream. When you go to sleep at night, and you can recall your dreams, there are usually moving pictures, images, sensations, and even thoughts or words. When you are creatively visualizing something out of the dream state, you are activating your higher mind and deeper consciousness.

There are plenty of people who already know how to do this and have always known how to close their eyes and imagine a far off and fantastical landscape full of whatever comes to mind. With a little practice, it can become even more detailed and elaborate, and you will find a greater opening with your capabilities with your psychic visions and ability to see beyond what is visible to the naked eye.

It is this skill that will help you see your chakras more clearly and be more open to understanding the visions that come up or resurface from past experiences so that you know what you need to let go of clearly. The path of awakening the third eye can be advanced when you practice this technique. Here are the simple guidelines to follow when you are practicing creative visualization:

1. Be open to anything that might surface without judgment or criticism.

2. Let go of thought patterns and cycles that you might easily get stuck in (ex: "I can't," "that isn't real/possible," "It doesn't even make any sense," etc.).

3. Teach yourself your own methods and avoid looking online or in books for a guide to help you connect with your third eye. The point is that you are connecting to your own unique intuition and identity.

4. Visualize things simple at first and then more elaborately as you get better at seeing the minute details.

5. Practice traveling to other "inner landscapes" and worlds to help show yourself the metaphorical and symbolic path that you need to travel.

6. Design your worlds to be places that you can return to over and over again to help yourself along your healing path.

7. Use your thoughts and feelings to direct the course of your creative visualization. It will help you to better identify what chakras will need the most healing, balance, or strengthening.

These simple guidelines are just to give you a platform to begin your own creative work. The journey of awakening the third eye is unique to the individual and will be different for everyone. It is important not to get too boxed into other people's views or perspectives about the "right" or "wrong" way to open your third eye (or any other chakras, for that matter).

Creative visualization is a portal to help you understand your own inner truth as well as to finding your path to universal consciousness and enlightenment. It isn't an easy road to travel, and as you will see in the next chapter, psychic awareness is not always a picnic.

Power of Psychic Awareness Through the Third Eye

There are no limits to what the human mind is capable of. We are only limited by our beliefs and ideas about what it all is supposed to be or look like. Awakening, the third eye asks you to let go of all of your preconceived notions of reality and to step into a new way of seeing all life on the planet.

The power of psychic awareness will make it challenging for you to know anything the way that you knew it before. It causes a great shift in your ability to "see" and "know" the truth about all areas of your life, which will, in turn, cause a lot of change, even when it is uncomfortable. You may not know it yet, but when you begin to ascend into your psychic knowledge, you will look at your world with a new set of eyes, and it will suddenly feel like everything you are doing in your life right now is "off" and needs to change or be resolved.

This great transformation happens very quickly, and many people will even avoid the cost of letting it unfold naturally out of fear of such a big life change or shift in consciousness and identity. There are certainly ways that you can help this experience unfold in a healthier and more comfortable way and here are just a few tips to help you understand that process:

1. Give up anything that no longer makes you feel like yourself.
2. Look for ways to explore your psychic awareness by listening to your inner codes and messages that come up. It is your intuition and inner knowing speaking to you. Keep a journal or a record of these psychic thoughts.
3. Bring yourself into a state of trance or meditation on a daily or regular basis to help you expand your consciousness more effectively.

4. Take a moment to listen to your gut reactions and instincts before you make a choice or speak any words to someone or yourself.
5. Denial is not a helpful tool, and so if you ask these questions and receive a response, do not deny it, no matter how far-fetched it may seem.
6. Collaborate with other methods of psychic practice, such as divination, scrying, tarot card reading, crystal empowerment of the third eye, etc.
7. Release any beliefs that suggest that being psychic isn't real or true.

The moment you begin to embrace your ability to just "know" you are giving yourself the opening to awakening your psychic abilities more than ever before. What are those psychic abilities? They manifest differently for everyone, but here is a list of some possibilities:

- Prophetic dreams and prophecies
- The ability to see what is about to happen as it is about to happen
- Welcoming the presence of spirit guides and other "ethereal helpers."
- Clairvoyance and clairsentience

- Being able to predict possible outcomes in a detailed way
- Journeying in mind to other dimensions of reality, or astral travel
- Being able to speak to energies on the "other side."
- Reading auras and being able to see the light and coloration of the auras
- Being able to read another person's energy and interpret what they are not saying out loud
- Telepathy
- And more!

Psychic awareness takes a lot of personal growth, stamina, and ability to see beyond the third dimension of reality. It can take you years to uncover the depths of your psychic powers and path, and if you put in the work to truly know yourself in this way, then you can advance your soulful awakening even faster than if you just did a few things here and a couple of things there. Enlightenment and awakening are not an easy thing to accomplish, and the next section will briefly cover that.

Understanding Enlightenment

Enlightenment simply means that you are awakening to your whole light source and power as a person. It is a connection to the universally divine energies inherent in all things and all nature. You don't have to be a yoga guru or someone who lives and breathes the philosophies of Eastern religions in order to know enlightenment. It is a different path for every person with different ways of traveling throughout life.

There are a lot of ways that people will feel confused about what enlightenment is because they are looking for perfection. It is not a state of perfection that equals enlightenment, but rather a state of truth within your own being. If you are resistant to your own truth, then you are not likely to become fully enlightened, and in order to get to that connection with yourself, you have to let go of what you think and believe that the world wants you to be. You can live your whole life exhausting your true purpose by trying to fit in the way other people do or try to.

Enlightenment is a growth experience, and it will never fit into a list of rules or a checklist. It is an ongoing process that delivers you to your highest and purest form of consciousness and even that required continuous fine-tuning and exploration. There really is no endpoint to the journey of self-discovery, and it will only limit you if you think, feel or believe that if only you could just make it that point, everything will be great forever.

It simply won't work that way, and having an awakened mind means that you are already in awareness of that simple truth and reality. Your third eye and your psychic ascension is the path that opens you to becoming enlightened and working forward toward living your life by your inner light and source energy. And that is really what healing the chakras and awakening is all about in the first place. The next chapter will expand upon the concept of an enlightened soul and why the vibration of love is one of the highest and lightest forms of energy available to all of us.

Chapter 10: The Practice of Love and Positive Vibration

Love is the answer, or so they say. Have you ever had an experience in your life when you were NOT asking for love on some level? The best way to explain the vibration of love is to help you remember your own experiences with a time in your life when you felt it. Yes, love can have a painful side, but what about the feeling of love that makes you glow, that makes you want to stand up and sing, or run around the block 15 times?

The vibration of love is very high, bright, and light. It is no wonder that people are always searching for it in some form or another. Even people who are rejecting love at every turn are actually showing off just how desperately they need or want it underneath the tough façade.

The energy of the heart chakra is where you can actually fully begin your chakra healing journey. When you consider that your health and happiness depends on the frequency of your inner chakra system, imagine how wonderful it will feel when you embrace it all from the perspective of love.

Self-Love and Awakening the Chakras

Too many of us are trying so hard to act out our need for love, demanding it from others and worried, fretful, or depressed when someone doesn't love us for exactly who we are, and the answer to that dilemma is so simple: practice loving yourself first. It should go without saying, but sadly, so many people are never taught the self-love tools that make for a secure and confident individual.

Think of it this way: when you are able to love yourself unconditionally, then you will be able to fully answer the energy of yourself and let yourself potentially open to your own source of truth and power, thereby deeply connecting you to the ageless love you have always wanted to know. On top of that, the love you have for yourself is how you are better able to love the other people in your life, including strangers on the street or honking at you in traffic.

There is a difference between self-love and egotism. It can be a major part of your awakening soul journey to unravel and unfold your ego-mind so that your love is coming from a healthy balance and a place of universal consciousness, not egotistical behaviors or narcissism. Sometimes people get confused about what it means to be incredibly loving and kind to yourself and what it is to boast or have an arrogance about everything you think, feel, and do.

Self-love is about knowing that it is okay to have flaws and to love even those parts of yourself. Self-love is about never rejecting who you are, no matter where you are in growth experience. Self-love is about rekindling your deepest purpose and passion so that you are living your life to its fullest without fear or criticism.

People all over the world struggle with loving themselves, and what do you think would happen if everyone did? What the world be like if everyone was capable of loving themselves without conditions?

The world needs you to love yourself fully, and that is a large part of what chakra healing is all about. When you are preparing to go on this journey, it helps to start from a loving place. Having a personal life that allows you to be who you are and live by your own rules is part of the experience, and after you begin to accept that you have all of the love you need from within, then you can truly heal what needs to be healed without searching for it outside of yourself.

The love that is reflected back to you from your own higher knowing is what will guide you more deeply on your path to awakening and soulful enlightenment. There are certain things to avoid during the practice of self-love, and some of those things include:

- Talking about yourself negatively, whether in your mind or out loud
- Using anything hurtful to harm yourself physically
- Taking out your frustrations about your life on yourself by using negative language or name-calling (you are stupid, horrible, incapable, etc.)
- Doing things regularly that you know make you feel bad about yourself
- Using substances to try and control your feelings or to cope with them
- Shaming or blaming yourself for things out of your control
- Creating a sense of guilt about anything you feel like you haven't done "right."
- Accusing yourself of being a problem or "the" problem
- Telling yourself, you don't have a life worth living
- Believing that you are unworthy of the things that you want

- Creating an attitude of resentment toward yourself for having not already "figured it out."

These are just some of the examples of where your mind and emotions can take you when you are against practicing self-love. Instead of these harmful and toxic pathways, try some of these ideas instead:

- Congratulate yourself daily for something you have done, whether big, small, routine, anything.
- Tell yourself one really nice and loving thing per day (ex: "I am looking brighter and brighter", or "I feel good about the ways that I have taken good care of myself today" or "I have a beautiful soul, and I deserve to shine brightly").
- Offer yourself a gift of some kind, even if it isn't for any reason in particular.
- Do things that help you to feel productive and goal-oriented.
- Get a good night's sleep on purpose.
- Accept yourself.
- Use affirmative language to help yourself through challenging or difficult life moments.

- Embrace that you are exactly where you need to be in your life right now.
- Keep track of your progress so that you can see how much you have grown.
- Create boundaries with other people or energies in your life that cause you to feel "less than."
- Enjoy some well-deserved relaxation and rest.
- Do something fun and enjoyable that you don't normally do but really like.

Sometimes in our lives, we get too bogged down within our negative mentalities, and the only way to successfully shift out of that consciousness is to think and feel differently about yourself. You have to start somewhere, and these little hints and tips show what you can avoid and what you can start doing to activate more love in your life.

The truth is, no one can love you better than you can, and when you love yourself from the inside out, you can then give all of that love to the world around you and spread that higher love vibration where it is needed the most.

Love from the Inside Out

The practice of love and positive vibration doesn't stop with you. Loving yourself is only the beginning of what love aspires to do and change in this world. There are so many of us, and we all need to have our own unique story of life. For some, it is part of their story to go through their whole lives never really knowing the true force of what love can do. For others, their story is to bring more love to the world because of their own path to discovering what love really is to us all.

When you are opening and awakening your chakras, you are already in the act of love. It is incredibly thoughtful of you to decide that you are ready and want to heal. That is a tough call to make sometimes, and it can take over your whole life as you begin to travel the steps of chakra healing and awakening. The results of choosing to positively shift your vibration are that you can feel whole and like you are capable of living by your own purpose and truth, but you will also inspire others to do so.

Positive and negative energy can carry far into the world, and if you are radiating the positive vibration of love for yourself and others, you will connect that energy to everything that is around you. Some people might be very resistant to your loving nature because they haven't learned how to fully love themselves yet, but you can certainly inspire someone else to look more deeply at their own love story with life when you are radiating and emitting that vibration.

The theories of the chakras and the way that they emit frequencies are still being studied by science, but you don't need science to prove that this is a true reality. Think about how it feels when you are really sad, and someone gives you a hug to console you. It changes your vibration and helps you to feel more uplifted. Consider how it feels on a really bad day when your coworker brings you a cupcake to show you that they know you are down and to offer you some solace in a tough moment.

All of these simple, loving acts can transform the energy that surrounds it. When you are able to offer love like that to yourself and to the world around you, you improve and maintain, not just your own chakra system and frequency, but possibly that of others as well, spreading the love all around with every moment of the day.

Think about it: your love vibration is what changes you and what changes the world around you. It is the most positive frequency you have, and if you want to really make a difference in your own life or someone else's, then practice the powerful vibration and positive energy of love.

Chapter 11: Testimonials About Chakra Healing

So many people today are embracing the powerful energy of healing from within by using methods to clear the chakras. You are one of the thousands and potentially millions of people who are working to heal, balance, awaken and strengthen the chakras. See for yourself what some people have been saying about their own experiences...

I had never heard of chakras before until I started taking a yoga class with one of my friends. I did yoga for almost a year until another friend of mine showed me a book she had about Kundalini Awakening. I read through it and tried some new practices and techniques to open my chakras even more. It was like nothing I had ever experienced before and felt really hard to explain or describe to anyone I knew. I felt like I could hear and see things more clearly, and like my skin would tingle when I was opening my chakras. It felt like I was vibrating underneath my skin. I am still on a profound journey with it all and am staying focused on a new practice to keep my eyes open along with my chakras. - Denise, 29

My boyfriend asked me to do some drugs with him one night, and I wasn't really feeling up to it. We had been getting high since we had gotten together and broken up a lot, too. When we got high, something different happened to me that had never happened before. I felt like my whole body woke up and like a hear a voice in my mind tell me to stop getting stoned and face my problems. It was so clear like there was someone in the room shouting it into my ear, but it was just in my head. I woke up and felt like I had to get out of there. I left, and I started getting clean, and I went to a local Buddhist temple to ask some questions. I was shown how to meditate, and it woke me up even more. I was skeptical at first of why I heard that voice, but then I was told by the instructor that I was waking up and hearing my true voice and not to avoid it, that I should listen. I had battled with drug addiction and alcoholism for most of my life, and when I was deep in meditation, connecting to my true voice, I felt more alive and like "me" than I had ever felt before. It took some time to get used to myself after all the years of covering myself up with booze and drugs, but it was worth it. - Jeremiah, 33

My mother had a stroke and was in hospital for weeks. I was basically living there with her and found out while

I was in the hospital that I had cervical cancer. My whole life was falling apart, and I couldn't believe it. I got so depressed I couldn't get out of bed, not even to help my mother through her recovery. My sister flew into town to help us out, and when she arrived, she booked me an appointment to see a Reiki Master. She laid me on a table and immediately knew, without me telling her, that I was sick. She said I had the energy of cancer. I asked her how she could have possibly known that I had just been diagnosed and she told me that it was the power of reading and seeing other people's energy. When I felt her Reiki session, it felt like her hands were moving the energy around in my body, but she almost never touched me with her hands. It was amazingly relaxing, and she showed me ways I could practice on myself at home. I took a few Reiki classes and discovered how much I had been neglecting my own energy. I started doing self-healing chakra, releasing work, all day sometimes, to help me with my cancer. I even practiced with my mom to help her with her stroke, and she recovered very well after I started helping her energy heal. I went back to the doctor's office for some tests, and he said that my cancer had already started to go into remission. I couldn't believe it. He asked me if I had changed anything an I told him about Reiki. He didn't really feel like it was possible for me to heal myself like that, but I told him that it was what had happened to change my life. I am still cancer-free, and I perform Reiki on myself regularly to stay in balance with my energy. - Louise, 48

Conclusion

Thank you for making it through to the end of *Chakra Healing for Beginners: The Complete Guide to Opening Your Third Eye, Awakening and Finding Balance Within Your Chakras Through Guided Meditation*, and let's hope it was informative and able to provide you with all of the tools you need to achieve your goals whatever they may be.

The next step is to put all of these tools into practice. Give yourself all of the space and time that you need to make this journey work well for you. You may have to make some changes to your diet and your regular "movement" routine. You may decide that you want to use mire crystals and gemstones to ignite your journey. Practicing yoga, as well as breathing and concentration or meditation exercises, will definitely get you on the right track to feeling open to awakening your chakra system.

Remember that all of your experiences will be unique to your healing discoveries. Try not to make too many comparisons to how other people's lives look when they go through an awakening journey. Focus on you and what you need to do in order to find true alignment with your own energy and purpose.

All of the chakra healing tools in this book will help you to stay open to what you can do to make great changes and shift in your energy. You may need to start slowly and work your wat up over time, or you may already be feeling the pull to make some major life changes that will help you to become well and ready for whatever comes your way on the chakra healing journey.

If you are feeling skeptical about chakra healing will do for you, give yourself two months of focused work on your own chakra system. Use the meditations and yoga poses form this book to get you started and then slowly incorporate other changes, like getting some herbal remedies to help cleanse your physical body, or some small crystals to lay on your third eye to help it open and awaken more.

There are so many useful tools and techniques in this book that are perfect for any beginner and will help you find all of the right openings you need to connect with your powerful healing journey. You can listen to other people talk about how to heal the chakras, or you can start using these methods right away to help you ignite your personal path to healing from within.

I hope you found this book useful and helpful on your road to discovering more about the chakras. The journey doesn't have to end here, and you can make it exactly the one you want it to be when you continue to use these simple tools and guidelines. May your healing path be full of enlightenment!

Finally, if you found this book useful in any way, a review on Amazon is always appreciated!

Lightning Source UK Ltd.
Milton Keynes UK
UKHW020639011220
374435UK00012B/948

9 781801 259460